D0982481

To Ken

A CALL FOR PEACE

地球憲法第九条

Oct. 1. 1997
Toru Kataoka
(JAPAN)

Distributed in the United States by Kodansha America, Inc.,
114 Fifth Avenue, New York, N.Y. 10011, and in the United
Kingdom and continental Europe by Kodansha Europe Ltd.,
95 Aldwych, London WC2B 4JF. Published by Kodansha
International Ltd., 17-14, Otowa 1-chome, Bunkyo-ku,
Tokyo112, and Kodansha America, Inc.

ISBN 4-7700-2062-7
97 98 99 00 10 9 8 7 6 5 4 3 2 1

A CALL FOR PEACE
The Implications of Japan's War-Renouncing Constitution

[著] TEXT
チャールズ M. オーバビー
Charles M. Overby

[訳] TRANSLATION
國弘正雄
Kunihiro Masao

[写真] PHOTOGRAPHS
桃井和馬
Momoi Kazuma

地球憲法
第九条

講談社インターナショナル
KODANSHA INTERNATIONAL

目次

Contents

この青い緑の星を守るために
「憲法第九条」
を世界中の人たちに捧げます。

今、地球上の全て
―大気、水、土、そし
て多様な生命が、本
書で展開する桃井和
馬の写真のように、未
来から奪い去られよ
うとしています。

この危機を救うのは
「地球憲法
　　第九条」
です。

The only way to save this planet is to spread the message of "Article 9 of the Japanese Constitution" among all the people in the world.

At this moment, everything on the planet—the atomosphere, water, earth, and all forms of life—runs this risk of being robbed of its future, as illustrated by Kazuma Momoi's photographs.

"Article 9 of the World Constitution"

can save us all from coming danger.

(Phot. courtesy Dandy Photo, Tanji Yasutaka.)

新しく鉄砲がつくられ、新しく軍艦が進水し、新しくロケットが発射されること、これは食べるものがなくて飢えているのに、着るものがなくて寒いのに、人々からさらに何かを奪い去ろうということに他ならない。
　武装された世界が費消しているのは金銭だけではない。全世界の働く人々の汗を、科学者たちの才能を、子どもたちの希望を使いつぶしているのである。これは真の意味における生き方などと呼べる代物ではない。戦雲のもとにおいては、これは人類が鉄製の十字架にかけられているに均しい。

ドワイト・D・アイゼンハワー大統領による
1953年のアメリカ新聞編集者協会での講演

Every gun that is made, every warship launched, every rocket fired signifies, in the final sense, a theft from those who hunger and are not fed, those who are cold and are not clothed. This world in arms is not spending money alone. It is spending the sweat of its laborers, the genius of its scientists, the hopes of its children …. This is not a way of life at all in any true sense. Under the cloud of war, it is humanity hanging on a cross of iron.

President Duright D. Eisenhower in a speech before the American Society of Newspaper Editors in 1953

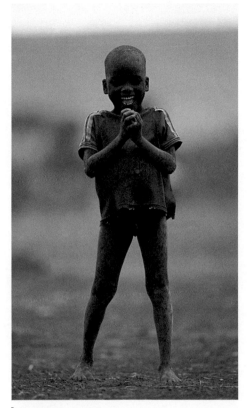

チャド。
Chad.

第九条 ― ARTICLE 9

1. 日本国民は、正義と秩序を基調
Aspiring sincerely to an international peace

とする国際平和を誠実に希求し、
based on justice and order, the Japanese people

国権の発動たる戦争と、武力によ
forever renounce war as a sovereign right of the

る威嚇又は武力の行使は、国際
nation and the threat or use of force as means

紛争を解決する手段としては、永
of settling international disputes. In order to

久にこれを放棄する。　2. 前項の
accomplish the aim of the preceding paragraph,

目的を達するため、陸海空軍その
land, sea, and air forces, as well as other war

他の戦力は、これを保持しない。
potential, will never be maintained. The right of

国の交戦権は、これを認めない。
belligerency of the state will not be recognized.

難民キャンプ。12月24
日 クリスマスイブ。(エ
チオピア)

Refugee camp on
Christmas Eve.
Ethiopia.

精神を病んだかっての
戦士。(アンゴラ) ▶

A former soldier still
suffering from the
agony of war (Angola).

放射能防護服をまとった男
性。(アメリカ、ハンフォード)
アメリカ、ワシントン州の砂漠
の中に、世界最大の核関連施
設ハンフォードがある。現在、
1万8000人がそこで核廃棄物
処理にあたっている。

A man wearing radiation
protective gear (Hanford,
Washington).
Located in the desert in the
state of Washington,
Hanford is the world's
largest nuclear complex. At
present it has 18,000 people
working on the disposal of
nuclear waste.

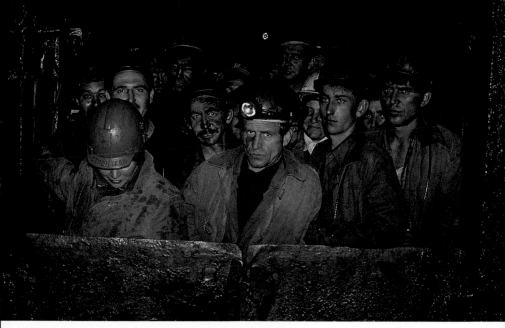

月3000円の給料をもらうため、彼らはエレベーターに乗り、地下500メートルにもぐる。設備が整っていないため、塵肺に苦しむ人が多い。（ウクライナ、クリボイログ）

For a monthly salary of some $30, these men descend in an elevator over 500 yards into the depths of the earth. Due to poor facilities, many suffer from pneumoconiosis. (Krivoi Rog, Ukraine).

アマゾンの開拓移民の家中の壁に貼りめぐらされた雑誌の広告。物があふれる都会への憧れか。

The walls of a pioneer family in the Amazon is plastered with advertisements from magazines, perhaps showing their attraction to the wonderful amenities of city life.

森で捕えられた象は鎖につながれ、「人のためになる象」になる。（インドネシア、スマトラ島）▶

These elephants, caught in the woods, have been chained until they become "elephants that works for people." (Sumatra, Indonesia)

海に廃棄された原子力船や原子力潜水艦。（ロシア、ムルマンスク）

Nuclear-powered ships and submarines discarded in the sea. (Murmansk, Russia)

栄養失調で病院に入院していたソマリア難民の子ども。
死を待つだけのその視線は透明だった。

A child hospitalized with malnutrition in Somalia.
Facing death, his gaze seems translucent.

内線当時のペルー、ジャングル地帯にて。

In the jungle in Peru during a period of internal warfare.

ユダヤ人をはじめ、ヨーロッパ諸国の400万人以上の人々が、
強制労働や毒ガスによって殺された。（アウシュビッツ強制
収容所の建物の中で）

Over 4,000,000 Jews and other Europeans died in labor
camps or were killed by poison gas during World War II.
(Inside the Auschwitz concentration camp)

謝辞

　私はこの本を、戦争を知りしかも私に希望を与えてくれた2人の佳人に捧げたい。1人は故人となられた市岡久さん、あと1人はいまもお元気な櫛田フキさんである。

　この本はまた自国をして憲法9条を尊重させようと願っている1億2500万人もの日本国民のものでもある。(1) 第9条の会、(2) 平和憲法（前文・第9条）を世界に拡げる会、(3) 平和カードの波運動、(4) 湯川スミ夫人の率いる世界連邦建設同盟、(5) 日本YWCAの女性会員、(6) 憲法9条——世界へ未来へ連絡会、(7) 憲法9条への希望をわれわれと共有する多くの団体の皆さん、(8) それに、交戦権という主権国家の権利の明確な放棄たる73語から成る憲法9条についてほとんど耳にしたことがないであろう地球上の約54億人以上もの人々、に対しても捧げられる。

　理解と激励とを示してくれた妻のルース、また私に多くを教えてくれた3人の娘たちに感謝したい。私はこの本を、不幸にしてこの世に生まれ出なかった1人の孫を想い、4人の現存する孫たちと全世界のすべての幼な児や若者のために書いた。彼らが戦争の悲惨や愚かしさなどを経験することなく、公正に支えられた平和な世界に成人してくれることを願ってである。

　勝守寛夫妻なしには、第9条の会は生まれ得なかったであろう。彼らこそは第9条の会の礎石であるとともに駆動力といえる。お2人がいままでに示してくれた励ましと支えとは不可欠であり、ふかく感謝する。

　このような本を1冊考えてみては、と提案してくれた講談社インターナショナルの編集者、浦晋亮氏にもお礼申し上げる、この本が生まれるに当たっての同氏の辛抱と理解と助力に対してである。

　私の年来の友人かつ助言者で、言葉の芸術家たるジム・マリーの執筆面での助力、それに妻のルースが、執筆のいくつもの段階で何度も読みかえしいろいろな助言をしてくれたことにも感謝する。私の歴史に関する専門家たるロバート・ウィーリーほか何人かの大学関係者にも、その励ましに対しお礼申し上げる。また最後になったが卓れた議会人で同僚、かつ堪能な語学者たる國弘正雄氏が翻訳の事にあたってくれたことにも多くを負っている。

Acknowledgments

I dedicate this book to two elegant Japanese women who have known war and who have given me hope—the late Hisa Ichioka and the very active Fuki Kushida.

This is also for the many millions of Japanese men and women who want their nation to honor Article 9 of their constitution. It is for the many Japanese supporters of (1) the Article 9 Society, (2) the Society for the Globalization of the Peace Constitution (Preamble and Article 9), (3) the Women's Peace Postcard Movement, (4) the United World Federalists of Japan under the leadership of Sumi Yukawa, (5) the Women of the Japan YWCA, (6) the Peace Constitution League, (7) the many other organized groups who share our hopes for Article 9—and (8) this is for the billions of Earth's people, most of whom have never heard of Japan's eloquent seventy-three word renunciation of the sovereign right of war—Article 9.

I am grateful to my wife, Ruth, for her understanding and encouragement, and to our three daughters from whom I have learned much. I write this for our four living grandchildren and in memory of the little one who didn't make it—and for all the world's children and youth, with the hope that they might "become" in a world of peace with justice, and without experiencing the brutality and absurdity of war.

Without Hiroshi and Megumi Katsumori there would be no Article 9 Society. Hiroshi and Megumi are what I call the foundation of our Article 9 Society and its driving engines. Their encouragement and support has been absolutely essential and is deeply appreciated.

Thanks to Kodansha editor, Kuniaki Ura, for his suggestion that we consider a book such as this—and for his patience, understanding and help in its birth.

Thanks also to Jim Murray, my long-time friend, advisor, and word artist, for his editorial assistance, and to Ruth for her several readings and suggestions at various stages of the manuscript. I am grateful to Robert Whealey, my history resource colleague, and to several other Athens friends for their encouragement. Last but not least I am indebted to distinguished legislator, colleague, and excellent linguist, Masao Kunihiro, for his crafting of the Japanese translation.

オーバビーさんが組織する「第9条の会」はアメリカの有力紙誌に、「憲法第9条」を紹介する意見広告を出しました。

---

73 Honorable and Eloquent Words for World Peace

TO
Citizens of the world

DATE
The 50th Anniversary of the end of World War II—1995

SUBJECT
A Gift from Japan

more—just as do writers like Joyce and Faulkner. Though respected by everyone, Oe is now not as widely read as Yoshi-moto, even in Japan.

Oe began writing early. By the time he completed his first novel, *Nip the Buds,*

Masao Miyoshi holds the Hajime Mori Chair in Literature at the University of California, San Diego. Among his books are Off Center (Harvard) and As We Saw Them (Kodansha America).

... juvenile hall are being trade for the protection of the good from these delinquent boys, an nids, to a remote mountain vill on their arrival a plague fright frightening all the villagers, w don their homes and leave the hind, together with an orphan Korean boy who has been sh army deserter. These abandon try to live together, stealing survival and gradually learning in a network of friendships. Fo the pestilence does not spread.

73 Honorable and Eloquent Words for World Peace

TO: Citizens of the world

DATE: The 50th Anniversary of the end of World War II — 1995

SUBJECT: A Gift from Japan

As we commemorate this 50th anniversary of the end of World War II, we might reflect on a gift from Japan called Article 9. One of the world's greatest but little-known treasures, Article 9 arose like a Phoenix out of WW II's flames and holocausts.

Article 9 renounces war as a sovereign right of the nation and as a means of settling international disputes. In its English translation it has but 73 honorable and eloquent words for world peace:

Article 9: *"Aspiring sincerely to an international peace based on justice and order, the Japanese people forever renounce war as a sovereign right of the nation and the threat or use of force as a means of settling international disputes.*

"In order to accomplish the aim of the preceding paragraph, land, sea, and air forces, as well as other war potential, will never be maintained. The right of belligerency of the state will not be recognized."

Created by the victors and the vanquished of WW II, Article 9 was given a home in Japan's new post-war constitution which went into effect on May 3, 1947. Japanese people now celebrate May 3rd as their "Constitution Day."

Article 9's new principles for international peace and justice grew from the Paris Peace Pact of 1928, the United Nations Charter of 1945, and the disaster of two world wars. As could nothing before in all of history, Article 9 reflected the grim reality of nuclear weapons.

War is Inappropriate

War is an inappropriate method for trying to settle disputes, international or otherwise. We learn anew from the world's contemporary ethnic-tribal-religious conflicts that military force or people trained as soldiers cannot resolve these disputes.

We need to try something new. Open dialogue facilitated by persons trained and skilled in nonviolent conflict-resolution must become our new models for settling disputes, preventing war, and restoring peace.

Recent encouraging examples of nonviolent conflict-resolution include — Norwegian efforts to bring Palestinian and Israeli people to talk with, rather than kill one another — the metamorphosis of the new South African government — the current talking rather than killing in Ireland — and former President Carter's non-governmental (NGO) involvement on the Korean peninsula, in Haiti and elsewhere.

Article 9 Belongs to All of Us

Article 9 is no longer Japan's alone. It belongs to all of us on earth who yearn for an end to the absurd waste and brutality of modern, high-technology warfare. We all have the responsibility to preserve this priceless treasure for future generations.

Unfortunately, Article 9 is presently under attack, both in Japan and internationally. We must help Japanese citizens to stand strong in urging their government to restore integrity to Article 9 and to demonstrate new paths of international leadership in war-prevention and non-violent means of conflict resolution as Japan's creative contribution for peace and justice in the world.

If you share our concerns, write to us and we will send you more information about our groups and our efforts.

If you wish to help, we can supply you with Article 9 postcards that you can send to world leaders asking their support for keeping Article 9 alive as a model for all nations and the United Nations, into the 21st Century and beyond.

The Society for Globalization of the Peace Constitution (Preamble and Article 9)
Nakano 5 24 16 201, Nakano-ku
TOKYO 164 JAPAN
Koshiro SHO   Fax 011 (81) 3 3389-0535
Narihiko ITO   Fax & Tel. 011 (81) 467 22 7554

Hiroshi KATSUMORI
The Article 9 Society
9-13, Ishiodai   2-Chome
KASUGAI, AICHI 487 JAPAN

Charles Overby
The Article 9 Society
P.O. Box 5564
ATHENS OH 45701-5564

序文

> われわれは兄弟姉妹として
> 生きていくことを
> 身につけなければならない。
> さもなければ、
> 愚者としてみな一緒に滅びてしまう。
>
> マーチン・ルーサー・キング2世[1]

　いまやわれわれは、第3一千年期のはじまりと日本国憲法の公布と施行の50周年を迎えている。このときにあたり、地球上これ以上有意義な戦争放棄条項はありえず貴重な宝物である、憲法9条に敬意を払うことはきわめて時宜を得たものである。憲法9条こそお互いにとっての「生き残りのための指針」たりうるからである。

　最初にお断りしておくが、この本に盛られた内容の多くは、むしろ皮肉な諷刺として捉えられるべきだ、という点である。50年もに及んだ冷戦分裂症状が終わったというのに、いまなお消費の拡大と生態系の破壊を事とする大国と呼ばれる国々は、地球上の全生命に優にピリオドを打つだけの、信じがたいほど破滅的な核・通常軍事技術のよろいで自らをまとっている。ところが他方では全世界の人々の必要は醜悪なほど充足されてはおらず、強制力によらない紛争処理もほとんどの場合無視されているのが現実である。一体こんな愚行を上まわる事態が想像できるだろうか。
　いわゆるGセブン[2]と呼ばれる大国も無責任きわまる。

Introduction

*"We must learn to live together as brothers,
or we will perish together as fools."*

Martin Luther King, Jr. [1]

As we approach the beginning of the third millennium and the 50th anniversaries of the promulgation and adoption of the Japanese Peace Constitution, it is most fitting that we pay tribute to Article 9 of that constitution—the priceless treasure that is earth's most significant legal renunciation of the sovereign right of war. Article 9 can be our "survival guide" for the new millennium.

Here at the beginning let me say that much of the material in this book would probably best be dealt with as satire. Can we imagine more ridiculous folly than that of over-consuming, ecosystem-destroying so-called great powers, poised at the end of fifty years of Cold War paranoia, still armed to the teeth with unbelievably lethal nuclear and other military technology capable of ending life on the planet—while real needs of people around the globe are grossly unmet, and non-violent conflict resolution is usually ignored?

How irresponsible that the Group of Seven nations[2] fail

というのは発展途上国における労働基準や環境基準を高めさえすれば、やみくもに人間や環境の搾取をつづける多国籍企業に待ったをかけるだけの力をもっているというのに、その力をさっぱり行使しようとはしないからである。またわれわれは、自分たちの生活様式が地球上のすべての人々の手に余ることを十分に知りながら、稀少な資源をやみくもに消費しつづけ、お互いの住処をせっせと汚しつづけている。こんな悲しい、不遜きわまりないことがあるだろうか。憲法9条という、普遍的かつ賢明で平和と公正にとって無限の価値をもつ宝物が、当の日本にあっても国際的にも批難の対象になっている。これほど愚かしいことがあるだろうか。残念ながら諷刺の文章を綴るのは私の十八番ではない。したがってその挑戦はこの創造的な分野に才のある方々に引き受けてもらうことにして私は身を退く。

　軍事力に溺れているかにみえる世界の指導者のほとんどは、この73語から成る、世界平和を目指す憲法9条という金言の英知を受け入れることができないでいる。第2次大戦で日本の軍国主義を打ち負かし、憲法9条の創成を助けたのはほかならぬ合衆国政府だったが、皮肉なことに、この50年というもの、憲法9条を後退させる上に一番大きく働いた外的な要因も、同じ合衆国政府であった。この後退の歴史の上で次々に一里塚となっていったのは、冷たい戦争、朝鮮戦争、ベトナム戦争、湾岸戦争、それに1996年4月の日米安保条約の再交渉ならびに拡大であった。

　この本で私が申し述べたいのはアメリカ流の軍事中心主義や国際関係での軍事力の位置づけは、今日のような国際情勢の一大転換期にあって、日本が範とすべき模範的なモデルではない、ということである。日本の皆さんが、憲法9条という誇るべきバッジを胸に、自

to use their power to elevate labor and environmental standards in developing countries so that multinational firms will not be as free to greedily exploit humans and the environment with impunity. How sad and arrogant that we blindly consume scarce resources and pollute our nests knowing full well that this lifestyle is not possible for everyone on the globe. What folly that this universally wise and priceless treasure for peace and justice, Article 9, is under attack both in Japan and internationally. Unfortunately, satire is not yet my domain of expertise, so I will have to leave this creative challenge to others who are gifted in that genre.

Most world leaders, addicted as they seem to be to military force, find it difficult to accept the wisdom of Article 9's seventy-three honorable words for world peace. Paradoxically the United States government, which helped in the creation of Article 9 after defeating Japanese militarism in World War II, has been the major significant external force for Article 9's erosion over the fifty years of its existence. Prominent milestones along this path of erosion have been the Cold War, the Korean War, the Vietnam War, the Persian Gulf War and the April, 1996, renegotiation and expansion of the US-Japan Security Agreement.

I therefore suggest in this book that the US model of militarism and military force in international relations is not an appropriate model for Japan to be emulating at this pivotal time in world affairs. I urge Japanese people to guide their government on a historic and independent new path as a

国政府に働きかけ、「良心的参戦拒否国家」として歴史的な新しい歩みを進め、世界平和と公正との日本的な貢献として強制力に依らない「代替奉仕サービス」の可能性を示していかれるようお奨めする。全世界の一般の人々が待ち望んでいるのは、相互間の不一致を解くにあたっては、いままでのように戦争の暴挙や強制力に依らず新しい手だてを講じていくことである。戦争と強制力を否定した憲法9条をもつ日本は新しいモデルを世界に提示する可能性と責務とを兼ね備えているのである。

ポール・ケネディが1987年に物した『大国の興亡』という書物からなにがしかの英知を手にしてしかるべきだろう。あの本にはいわゆる大国がその興亡の歴史にあって、自らの経済力の限界を超えて愚かしくも軍事的に背伸びしていったいきさつが縷々述べられている。[3] 新しい一千年期の初頭にあって、アメリカをはじめとする「大国」が、憲法9条を軽視するのではなく、日本に対し、逆に「大国」であるとはどういうことであるかについての新しい方途を大胆に提示するよう、強く働きかけるべきである。この方途とは、憲法9条を基盤とする、非軍事的な、国際関係での成功例の、それである。

私のこの本は、アメリカをはじめとする国々や国際連合が今後向かうべき理想としての憲法9条を、肯定的かつ希望をこめて描き出そうというものである。

アメリカといえどもケネディが明らかにした愚かしさや、大国にまつわる力の奢りから自由ではない。したがってこの本は私の母国たるアメリカ合衆国に辛口すぎるように時おりは聞こえるかも知れない。[4] アメリカは多くの健全で前向きな側面をもっており、私も一市民としてそのことを多としている。ただ多くの問題

"Conscientious Objector" nation demonstrating non-violent "alternative service" as its contribution to world peace and justice, with Article 9 as its badge of honor. In place of the brutality and violence of war, the world's ordinary people cry for something new for settling differences. Japan has the potential and challenge to offer a new model based on the war-and-violence-renouncing principles in Article 9, from which all nations might learn.

It is time that we recognize some of the wisdom from Paul Kennedy's 1987 book, *The Rise and Fall of the Great Powers: Economic Change and Military Conflict from 1500 to 2000*—namely that the "great-powers," in their rise and fall, exhibit considerable hubristic folly in extending themselves militarily beyond what their economies can sustain.[3] Here at the beginning of this new millennium the "great powers" (including the USA) rather than undermining Article 9, should strongly encourage Japan to boldly demonstrate a new course to what it means to be a "great power"—a course based on Article 9, a non-military mode of successful existence in international affairs.

This book is meant to be a positive and hopeful focus on Article 9 as an ideal toward which all nations, including the USA, and the United Nations should move as we enter the third millennium. Because America is not immune to the hubris-folly affliction identified by Kennedy and the arrogance of power that accompanies "great-power" status, this book may at times sound rather critical of my country, the USA.[4] America has many wholesome and positive dimensions for which I, as a citizen, am quite grateful. It also has

点をかかえていることも事実で、その持てる可能性を
フルに開花させるためには、これらの問題点への対応
が必要とされる。たとえば、『政治の意味：白茶けた時
代における希望と可能性の復権』という著書の中でマ
イケル・ラーナーは、今日のアメリカ文化における疎
外や白け、利己性や物質万能主義を論じている。[5] 彼が
もくろんでいるのは「政治の意味」をアメリカに打ち
立てることに他ならない、すなわち、それぞれの機構
の価値を決めていくのが、どの程度まで倫理や生態面、
愛情や慈しみの関係を最適化できるかであるような仕
組みを彼は「政治の意味」と呼んでいるのである。

　アメリカの軍事中心主義や国際関係における軍事力
優先政策を批判しても、私は決して個々のアメリカ兵
士を責めているのではない。彼らは政策遂行上の単な
る道具にすぎぬからである。彼らもまた、軍事力や戦
争、それへの準備こそが、望ましい社会活動の一環で
あるという、軍事中心的世界観の犠牲者なのである。
彼らはまた、その武器によって致命的な暴力を蒙った
無辜の相手とは別の意味の犠牲者である。というのは、
暴力こそが唯一の対応策という固定観念にがんじがら
めにされているばかりでなく、戦地から復員したあと
であらぬ被害を受けたことに気づき、軍務の結果とし
ての肉体的精神的被害者であることを官憲に訴えては
みたものの、納得してもらえぬ場合が少なくないから
である。現行の湾岸戦争後遺症をめぐる対立や、ベト
ナム戦争がらみのオレンジガスの被害問題、またアメ
リカによる核実験の最盛期、兵士が当の本人が知らぬ
間に実験的に放射能にさらされ健康上の被害を受けた
ことなどは、他ならぬアメリカ兵士自身が犠牲に供せ
られた具体的な事例である。

　私自身は自らを愛国者とみなしている。同じような

many problems that need to be addressed so that its potential might truly unfold. For example, Michael Lerner in his book *The Politics of Meaning: Restoring Hope and Possibility in an Age of Cynicism* discusses the alienation, cynicism, selfishness, and materialism of contemporary American culture.[5] He seeks to establish a "politics of meaning" in America where institutions will be judged according to how well they tend to maximize ethical, ecological, loving, and caring relationships in the culture.

When I criticize US policies of militarism and military force in international relations, I am not attacking individual soldiers who are the instruments by which these policies are implemented. Soldiers are also victims of a militarist world view that regards military force, war and the preparation for war as normal and desirable societal activity. Soldiers are victims in different ways than are the innocent recipients of the lethal violence delivered with their weapons. In addition to crippling from being inculcated with a mind-set that sees violence as the only way, soldiers learn of their victimization after they return from battle and find it difficult to persuade public officials that their military service caused damage to their physical and mental health. The current Gulf War health syndrome conflict in America, the agent orange health problems from Vietnam, and the nuclear radiation illness caused by soldiers being purposefully exposed to bomb radiation, as uninformed experimental subjects, during the peak of America's nuclear testing programs illustrate concrete forms of US soldier victimization.

I consider myself a patriot, along with millions of other

懸念を共有する何百万人という他のアメリカ人ととも
にである。われわれが望むアメリカとは、道義性や真
実、平和や公正をその力の中核におき、国際関係にお
ける真の意味での傑出したリーダーとして、その潜在
する可能性をフルに発揮できる、そのようなアメリカ
である。

　かのマーチン・ルーサー・キング師が、1963年の「私に
は夢がある」演説で、「独立宣言書」の1節を引き、その
希望を述べたごとく、われわれがアメリカに望むのも、よ
り高次の行動基準を設けてくれることなのである。黒人
への平等と公正を求め、同師はこのようにうたい上げた。

　　「私には夢がある。いつの日にかアメリカ人が独立
　　宣言書で『自明の理』とされた『すべての人間は
　　平等に造られている』という信条に身の丈を合わ
　　せ、それを実践してくれる、という夢がである」

　憲法9条の英知とともに、日本は非暴力的な紛争解決
と戦争防止の面で世界規模でのリーダーシップを発揮
する可能性をもっていると私が指摘するとき、アメリ
カもまたいつの日にかこの種のリーダーシップを発揮
してくれるようにという私の夢をもあわせ物語ってい
るのである。

　アメリカ政府と市民のかなりの部分があまりにもし
ばしば見せる軍事中心主義の考え方に禍いされ、戦争
防止と紛争解決のための、非軍事や外交など非暴力的、
非強制的な多くの手だてに、すっかり目がふさがれて
いるのは悲しい限りである。政治社会学者のマイケ
ル・マンは、いま日本に求められている挑戦の巨大さ
をわれわれに悟らせるような形で「軍事中心主義」と
いう言葉を定義してくれている。彼によれば「軍事中
心主義」とは「戦争や戦争準備をもって自然で望まし

Americans who share my concerns. We seek an America that might fulfill its promise and potential to be a truly outstanding leader in world affairs with morality, truth, and peace and justice, as centerpieces on its table of power.

We seek a higher standard for the USA as did Martin Luther King as he quoted from our Declaration of Independence in his 1963 "I Have A Dream" speech. In his search for equality and justice for black Americans, he said,

"I have a dream that one day this nation will rise up and live out the true meaning of its creed: 'We hold these truths to be self-evident; that all men are created equal.'"

When I suggest that Japan, with the wisdom of Article 9, has the potential to demonstrate world class leadership in non-violent conflict resolution and war prevention, I am also saying that I have a dream that America would one day show this kind of leadership.

The US government and a significant fraction of its citizens all too often exhibit an attitude of militarism that sadly blinds America to a multitude of non-military, diplomatic, and other non-violent modes of preventing war and resolving conflict. Michael Mann, a political sociologist, has defined "militarism" in a way that helps us sense the magnitude of the challenge here being asked of Japan. Mann sees militarism "as an attitude and a set of institutions which regard war and the preparation for war as a normal and desir-

い社会的活動とみなす考え方や一連の組織機構」[6]を指している。われわれが必要とするのは「軍事中心主義」をもって不自然にして望ましくない「社会的活動」とみなす新しい世界観なのだ。

とここまで述べてきて、1つ付け加えたいのは、このところアメリカ政府が折にふれ戦争防止や非強制的暴力的な紛争解決のために多少は国際的なリーダーシップを示そうとしている気配が感じられると、いう点である。北アイルランド、旧ユーゴスラビア、中米、それに朝鮮半島がらみで平和と非強制的な紛争解決にアメリカが見せている外交努力はその例である。だが、これらの外交努力の一部について、その真の動機がどこにあるのか、必ずしもはっきりしないのは残念である。たとえばボスニア和平交渉におけるアメリカ側のイニシアティブは、(1) NATOの存続理由が消失してしまった脱冷戦下の今日にあって、その存在理由をむりに引き伸ばし (2) ヨーロッパの入り口にアメリカ軍が片足をおきつづける、という2つの動機があるのでは、という臆測が行われている。

いま1つの矛盾は、一方で退役したアメリカ軍将兵をボスニアのイスラム軍の武装や訓練に用いるなど軍事力こそが「あるべき姿」と見ているのとはうらはらに、和平保証軍のトップが同地域におけるこの種の軍事力の増強はいかがなものかと懸念を口にしている、という事実である。これらの平和へのかかわりも、あるいは失敗に終わりかねないが、新しい一千年期における「大国」の役割、すなわち日本国憲法9条が内包する戦争と強制力防止の役割の、期待できる実例を提供している。

先進国による稀少資源の過大な消費と環境の無責任きわまる汚染とは、紛争の重要な要因たりうる。憲法

able social activity."[6] We need a new worldview that sees militarism as abnormal and undesirable social activity.

Having said the above, let me add that there are signs now and then of the US government appearing to demonstrate some international leadership for war prevention and non-violent conflict resolution. Illustrative are US diplomatic efforts for peace and non-violent conflict resolution in Northern Ireland, the former Yugoslavia, the Middle East, and the Korean peninsula. Unfortunately we cannot be quite sure what the motivations are for some of this activity. There is some speculation, for example, that US leadership in the Bosnian peace process has something to do with (1) keeping NATO alive in a post-Cold War world when its reason for existing seems over, and (2) keeping America's military foot in Europe's door. There is also the paradox of America seeing military force as "the way to go" in its arming and training of the Bosnian Muslim military using retired US military officers and men, while at the same time Implementation Force military leaders express concern at this additional military buildup in the region. All of the above involvements for peace could seriously unravel, and yet they do demonstrate hopeful examples of what should be the new millennium role of "great powers"—a role of war and violence prevention implied by Article 9.

The over-consumption of scarce resources and the irresponsible trashing of the environment by developed nations is

9条はまた、環境と折りあっていく上の「生き残り」の指針たりうる。もしも全世界の高度技術社会がその必要に目ざめ、資源の消費と環境破壊を最小限にとどめる技術やシステムを設計し創造することに全力投球するなら、資源不足のもたらす紛争の可能性は減殺されよう。私がGTBD、つまりは意図的なグリーン・テクノロジー、と呼ぶところのものである。高品質な製品を国際貿易場裡に提供してきた秀れた実績を思うと、日本がGTBDを通じて平和への非強制的非暴力的な貢献を示す恰好な存在であることははっきりしている。

アメリカがその武器の国際的な移転という凶々しさへの惑溺を乗り越えようとすれば、他者の助力は欠かせない。武器通商への惑溺は世界平和や公正にとってプラスではありえない。この武器移転といううとましい活動において、アメリカは全世界をリードしている。[7]アメリカ商務省をはじめ連邦政府の諸機関は、このところ世界をめぐり歩いては、アメリカの軍需産業の売りこみに狂奔、外国政府相手にアメリカ製兵器の販売促進にあたっている。これらの相手国の多くが途上国で、限られた財源を人殺し用のナンセンスに浪費する余裕など持ち合わせていないにもかかわらず、である。
日本が国際的な武器通商に大がかりに参加しないで済んだのも、ひょっとすると憲法9条のおかげであったかも知れない。これはきわめて前向きな現象である。日本国民はすべからく自国の指導者に、武器通商に参加しなかったことを誇りとするよう、また他の諸国が日本の例にならうよう、明確かつ威厳をもってこの方向を継続的に推進するよう求めていくべきである。アメリカとの今後の通商交渉にあって、その中心的な一部として、日本側代表がアメリカ側をかこいこみ、ア

a significant cause of conflict. Article 9 can also be our survival guide for making peace with the environment. If the world's high technology societies can rise to the occasion and commit themselves to design and create technology and systems that minimize resource consumption and environmental degradation, something I call "green technology by design" (GTBD), they might simultaneously reduce the propensity for conflict driven by resource scarcity. Japan's track record of creating high quality products for international trade uniquely equips her to demonstrate GTBD as one of her non-violent contributions for peace.

America needs some help in overcoming its addiction to the unsavory international weapons trade, an affliction that does not well serve the cause for world peace and justice. The US leads the entire world in this repugnant activity.[7] The US Department of Commerce and other US governmental bureaucracies circle the globe these days, pimping for America's weapons industries—promoting weapon sales to foreign governments, many in developing countries who can ill afford dissipating their limited resources on this kind of lethal nonsense.

Article 9 may have helped restrain Japan from major participation in international weapons trade. This is a most positive phenomenon. Japanese people should ask their leaders to be proud of their non-involvement in weapons trade and to promote around the globe, clearly and with dignity, this national behavior as an example for all nations to follow. As an integral part of future trade talks with America, Japanese negotiators might expect the US government to implement policies that will ultimately put US international weapons

メリカ政府が究極的に武器通商を根だやしにできるような政策の実施に踏み切らせ、やがてはこの無責任にして恥ずべき通商活動を世界規模でなくしてしまうことを考えてもよいのではないか。

　この新しい一千年期を迎えるにあたってお互いぜひとも日本国憲法によって導かれていこうではないか。世界平和と公正とを目指すこの73語から成る金言は、第2次大戦の業火と大量殺戮の中から不死鳥のごとくによみがえったものなのである。

trade into extinction, and thereby help to end this irresponsible and shameful international commerce worldwide.

Let us be guided on our paths in the new millennium by Article 9 of the Japanese Constitution, whose seventy-three honorable words for world peace and justice arose like a Phoenix out of the flames and holocausts of World War II.

註釈

1. 「ザ・ネーション」誌　1997年2月10日号、7ページ。

2. Gセブンとは英国、カナダ、フランス、ドイツ、イタリア、日本およびアメリカ合衆国の7ヵ国から成る。

3. ポール・ケネディ『大国の興亡：1500年から2000年に至る経済上の変化と軍事対決』1987年　ニューヨーク・ランダムハウス刊。日本語版は草思社より刊行。

4. J・ウィリアム・フルブライト『権力の奢り』1966年　ニューヨーク・ランダムハウス刊。日本語版は日本経済新聞社より刊行。
　　この書名ならびに著者のフルブライト上院議員をして本書をしたためさせた動機は、1964年のいわゆる「トンキン湾決議」の際に、リンドン・B・ジョンソン大統領によってまんまとワナにはめられた経験に起因する。この大統領と議会による決議が、実質的にアメリカのベトナム戦争大量介入への道を開いたのである。
　　第2次大戦の死者と破壊とに心を痛めた同議員は自らの名前を冠した国際交流計画を発足させ、世界的な平和と公正とを促進のための手だてとした。フルブライト交流計画が、これである。また1943年6月に当時若手議員だった同氏は、戦後にそなえて国際機関の創立を求める短い決議をアメリカ議会に提出、これが後の国際連合の前身となった。

5. マイケル・ラーナー『政治の意味。白茶けた時代における希望と可能性との復権』1966年　アディソン・ウエスレー刊。
　　ラーナーは今日のアメリカ文化における疎外、白け、利己性、物質万能主義を論じ、各機構の価値を判断するに際し、単なる生産性や効率を超えた新しい価値基準を設けるべきだとした。

6. ジョン・F・ハッチンソン『慈善の旗手たち：戦争と赤十字の勃興』6ページ。1996年ウェストビュープレス刊。

7. 「いま一つの軍備管理」　クリスチャン・サイエンス・モニター紙、1996年6月20日号、20ページ。
　　国際的な武器取り引きのうちアメリカの占める割合は約52%と、全世界の他のすべての国々の合計を上まわっている。悲しいことにアメリカ政府はこれらの取り引きに輸出助成金を付けることで、武器メーカーの利益率をかさ上げしている。一種の企業福祉政策といえるのではないか。

NOTES

1. *The Nation,* 10 February 1997, p. 7.

2. The Group of Seven nations are Britain, Canada, France, Germany, Italy, Japan, and the United States.

3. Kennedy, Paul, *The Rise and Fall of the Great Powers: Economic Change and Military Conflict from 1500 to 2000.* New York: Random House, 1987.

4. Fulbright, J. William, *The Arrogance of Power.* New York: Random House, 1966. The title of this book and Senator Fulbright's motivation to write it came from his having been deceived by President Lyndon B. Johnson's 1964 "Gulf of Tonkin Resolution"—an action by the president and the Congress that substantially accelerated US involvement in the Vietnam War. Fulbright, pained by the death and destruction of World War II, originated the US international people exchange program that bears his name, The Fulbright Program, as a vehicle to promote peace and justice around the world. As a junior member of Congress in June, 1943, Fulbright introduced a brief resolution for the establishment of a postwar international organization that ultimately became the United Nations.

5. Lerner, Michael, *The Politics of Meaning: Restoring Hope and Possibility in an Age of Cynicism.* Addison Wesley, 1996. Lerner discusses the alienation, cynicism, selfishness, and materialism in contemporary American culture, and sees the need to establish criteria beyond those of mere productivity and efficiency for judging the worth of institutions.

6. Hutchinson, John F., *Champions of Charity: War and the Rise of the Red Cross.* Westview Press, 1996, p. 6.

7. "The Other Arms Control," *The Christian Science Monitor,* 20 June 1996, p. 20. The US share of the international conventional weapons trade is more than all of the other nations of the world combined—some 52 percent. Sadly, the US government encourages these sales with export subsidies, a form of "corporate welfare," so as to improve arms makers' profitability.

CHAPTER

1

冷戦当時、アメリカとソ連の代理戦争に巻き込まれてしまったエチオピア。冷戦が終わったいま、銃を持つことが一人前の男の証と考えられるまでになった。▶

During the Cold War Ethiopia was sucked into a proxy conflict between the United States and the Soviet Union. Even now, long after the end of the Cold War, the sign of manhood is to have a weapon in your hand.

はじまり

BEGINNINGS

ここに居るわれわれに多くを求めはしない
ただある高みを求めはする
だから群衆があるいは賞賛を
またあるいは批難をと
とつおいつさせたときには
すべからく星のごときものを選んで
心をおちつかせ
生まじめでいるべきだろう

ロバート・フロスト
「星のごときものをこそ」[1]

　この本は、世界でもっとも有意義な戦争に対する法的な差し止め命令たる、日本国憲法9条への敬意をこめた、1つの主張をなすためのものである。[2] 第2次大戦の業火と大量殺戮（ホロコースト）の中からあたかも不死鳥のごとく、国際平和と公正への一連の新しい原則が生まれ、日本国憲法の第9条にその安住の場を求めた。勝者と敗者の双方によって日本国憲法に位置づけら

It asks little of us here.
It asks of us a certain height.
So when at times the mob is swayed
To carry praise or blame too far,
We may choose something like a star
To stay our mind on and be staid.

Robert Frost, *from*
"Take Something Like A Star"[1]

This is an advocacy book in tribute to the world's most significant legal injunction against war, Article 9 of the Japanese Constitution.[2] Arising like a phoenix out of the flames and holocausts of World War II, a set of new principles for international peace and justice found a home in Article 9 of Japan's Constitution. Placed in this constitution by the victors

れた戦争の放棄は、普遍的にしてかけがえのない宝物であり、お互いの未来へのモデルとして世界がこれを失うような勿体<ruby>勿体<rt>もったい</rt></ruby>ないことはできない。人間にとって不可避な争いごとを解決するために非暴力的な手段がありうることを示唆している憲法9条は、新しい時代におけるわれわれにとっての羅針盤であり生き残りのための指針たりうる。

第9条ならびに日本国憲法の前文にとっての先駆的な存在は、すでに1928年8月27日のケロッグ・ブリアン協定（いわゆるパリ条約）ならびに1945年6月26日に結ばれた国際連合憲章に見られる。ただ国連憲章が公布されたのは、原子爆弾が広島と長崎の2都市で多くの人々を蒸発、被曝、焼却する6週間以前で、日本国憲法が1947年5月3日に施行される2年近く前のことであった。したがって日本国憲法こそは、核新時代の恐るべき実態を反映している点で、他の従前の文書とは異なっている。

残念ながら憲法9条は世界でもっともよく保持された秘密といえる。というのは、世界のほとんどの人々の耳目に触れたことはなく、日本を含む世界の主要国のほとんどの指導者が育成させその趣旨を誇りをもって全世界に伝え、すべての国にとってのモデルとして生成発展させていくことに、それほど熱心とは見えぬからである。

そこでこの本が目指すのは、(1) 地球上のもっと数多くの人々が憲法9条に盛られた戦争放棄のみごとな諸原則に親しみ、それぞれの国の憲法や行動規範に同様な原則を取り入れさせるための努力をうながし、(2) その廃棄を目途とする国の内外の圧力に抗して、とくに若者を中心とする日本の一般市民が、憲法9条の真髄の賦活化に向かっていく努力を活気づけ、(3) 他の国々の人々をして日本国民のこの種の努力を勇気づけさせ、(4) もっとも名誉ある紛争解決の手段としての非暴力非軍事的な行動についての思考や討議や行動を刺戟し、(5)

and the vanquished, this renunciation of war is such a universal and priceless treasure that the world can ill afford to lose it
as a model for our future. Article 9, which implies that we
use non-violent means to resolve our inevitable conflicts, can
be our compass and survivor's guide to the new millennium.

Precursors to Article 9 and the Preamble of the Japanese
Constitution can be found in the August 27, 1928, Kellogg-
Briand Pact, the so-called Paris Peace Pact, and in the United
Nations Charter signed on June 26, 1945. However, the UN
Charter was signed six weeks before the Hiroshima and
Nagasaki nuclear bombs vaporized, irradiated, and incinerated
people, and almost two years before Japan's Peace Constitu-
tion went into effect on May 3, 1947. The Japanese Consti-
tution therefore reflects, as have no previous documents, the
new awful truth of the nuclear age.

Unfortunately, Article 9 is one of the world's best kept
secrets. Most people around the globe have never heard of it,
and most leaders of major nations, including Japan itself,
seem not very interested in proudly spreading its message to
the world or in nurturing it so that it can grow and thrive as a
model for all nations.

It is my hope that this book will help (1) to acquaint
many more Earth citizens with the beautiful war-renouncing
principles expressed in Article 9, and to stimulate them to
work for the adoption of Article 9 principles in their own
nation's constitutions and codes of conduct; (2) to energize
Japanese citizens, especially including the young, in their
efforts to restore Article 9's integrity in the face of domestic
and international pressure to destroy it; (3) to encourage persons in other nations to support Japanese people in these

憲法9条を前記のロバート・フロストの詩作がいう、われわれの共通の目標としての、星とみなすことを得せしめ、その諸原則を地球上の全国民にとっての生き残りのための規範たらしめる闘いの場で、「心をおちつかせる」ための努力に資することにある。

　1995年から97年にかけて、われわれは歴史上の多くの重要なできごとの50周年を迎える。第2次大戦という大災害の終結、1945年の国際連合の創設にともなう新しい希望、それに1946年11月3日に公布され、1947年5月3日に施行された第9条を含む日本国憲法がこれであり、憲法施行の5月3日はいまでは憲法記念日として日本の国民の祝日の1つになっている。

　冷戦が終わりいくつもの50周年を迎え、新しい一千年期に近づくにつれて、われわれが国家間の新しい関係のあり方について大胆に発想し、暴力の支配に代わるに法の支配をもってする方途を模索することは、火急でもあり時宜をも得ている。国家間における法の支配への不可欠な要素の1つは、国家主権の一部の放棄だが、それは憲法9条が主権としての交戦権を放棄したことにおいてみごとに実現を見ている。

　諸国家間の関係において何が可能でありうるかについて新しい展望や思考、それに行動様式についてのパラダイムの転換が緊急に求められるようになっている。戦争や戦争準備を自然で望ましい社会活動とみなす考え方や組織機構を離れ、この手の軍事中心主義を不自然かつ望ましくない社会活動とみなす新しい世界観へと移っていく、いまやその時なのである。[3]
　日本はその過去に、争いごとを解決するためのパラダイム

endeavors; (4) to provoke thinking about, discussion of, and action for non-violent, non-military modes of conflict resolution as the most honorable means; and (5) to help us see Article 9 as the star of Robert Frost's poem, toward which we might aim—to "stay our mind on" in our struggle to have its principles become the norm for all nations on Earth as our guide for survival in the new millennium.

In this period from 1995 through 1997 we celebrate the 50th anniversaries of many significant events in the course of history: the end of the cataclysm that was World War II, the new hope with the founding of the United Nations in 1945, and the promulgation of the new postwar Japanese Constitution with its eloquent Article 9, on November 3, 1946, which went into effect on May 3, 1947—a day that is now Japan's Constitution Day.

With the Cold War ended and at this time of 50th anniversaries, and as we approach the new millennium, it is urgently appropriate that we think boldly of new relationships between nations in which the rule of violence is replaced by the rule of law. One of the essential ingredients for a rule of law between nations is some yielding of state sovereignty as was accomplished in Japan with its Article 9 renunciation of the sovereign right to war.

This is a time that cries out for a paradigm shift to new visions and patterns of thought and action as to what might be possible in relationships between nations. This is a time for changing attitudes and institutions which regard war and the preparation for war as normal and desirable social activity to a new worldview that sees this kind of militarism as abnormal and undesirable social activity.[3]

At an earlier time in its history, Japan made a paradigm

を転換させた歴史をもっている。その『鉄砲を捨てた日本』の中でノエル・ペリンが描いているように、日本は鉄砲という高度に発達した武器を自発的に捨て、刀というより原始的な武器に回帰した。[4]冷戦という圧倒的な基調が消滅した今日こそ、憲法9条を栄誉ある証しとして胸に、世界規模でのリーダーシップを発揮し、従来、普通の国が通ってきた戦争と暴力という道程からギアを創造的に入れかえ、非暴力による国家間関係という新しい道程を切り開いていくべき時が到来した。

私の変身

　この本をなぜ私が書いたかについての理解の一助として、第2次大戦当時若き志願兵だった私が、どのような経緯を経て、今日、人間同士の不可避な対立抗争を非暴力非軍事的な手段で解決していくことを唱えるに至ったかを少しく申し上げたい。また、なぜ憲法9条の会を樹立させたかを述べ、その目標や目的を素描してみたい。

　私は1926年3月、モンタナ州はキャスケードで生を享けた。巨大なミシシッピー河がロッキー山脈から出て東に流れるところにある小さな村である。ノルウェー移民を両親に6人の子どもの1人として、1930年代の大恐慌の時代にモンタナ州東北部のレッドストーンという、たかだか人口150人ほどの町で少年期を送った。父はグレート北部鉄道会社で保線関係の職長職にあった。

　少年時代の私はどういうわけか空を飛ぶことに強い興味を抱いており、1943年には17歳でアメリカ空軍に志願し、翌44年に操縦士訓練のために現役入隊した。第2次大戦終了時には、B29の機関砲手養成所にあったので、もし第2次大戦が引

shift in the way it resolved its conflicts. As Noel Perrin describes in his book *Giving Up the Gun: Japan's Reversion to the Sword, 1543–1879*, Japan voluntarily chose to give up an advanced military weapon, the gun, for a more primitive one, the sword.[4] Perhaps the time has come, with the breakup of the dominant Cold War theme, for Japan to demonstrate world class leadership with Article 9 as its distinctive badge of honor, with a creative shift from age-old path of war and violence trod by ordinary nations to a new path of non-violent relations between nations.

My Metamorphosis

To help you understand this book and the reasons for my writing it, let me first share a little of my metamorphosis from a youthful World War II military service volunteer to my present status as an advocate of non-violent, non-military means for resolving our inevitable human conflicts. Let me also give my reasons for founding the Article 9 Society and outline its goals and objectives.

I was born in March, 1926, in Cascade, where the mighty Missouri River pours out of the Rocky Mountains and flows east. One of six children of immigrant Norwegian parents, I grew up in the 1930s depression years in Redstone, a small town of less than 150 people in northeastern Montana, where my father was a Great Northern Railroad track maintenance foreman.

As a child I somehow developed an intense interest in flying, which translated into enlistment in the US Air Corps in 1943 at the age of seventeen and active duty in 1944 scheduled for pilot training. The end of World War II found me in

き続いていたとすれば、かのカーティス・ルメイ将軍の率いるB29爆撃隊の一員として、日本の諸都市の焼き打ち作業に従った筈であった。

戦後、私はGIビルという名の復員兵への奨学資金を受け、ミネソタ大学で機械工学の教育を受けることができ、1950年6月には同大学から機械工学の学士号を受けた。[5] 学内の予備将校訓練講座 (R.O.T.C.) を終え、アメリカ空軍の少尉に任官した。

卒業後日ならずして朝鮮戦争が勃発、私は心ならずも現役に呼び戻された。空を飛びたいという少年時代の思いを保ち残していたこととて、ほどなく操縦者訓練学校に志願し、同校を終えるとほどなくB29の副操縦手として配属され、沖縄の嘉手納を基地に北朝鮮の目標に対する爆撃行動に従事した。

私の戦闘体験はささやかなものでしかなかったが私の胸中に1粒の種子を残し、年とともに理解と懸念という全くちがった木を育てていくに至る。暗闇にまぎれて地上5マイルの高度から70トンもの爆弾を投下し、無差別な殺人と破壊に手を染めたことで、生まれてはじめて、戦争という名の組織的な殺人と破壊にとって代わるもっと気のきいた紛争解決の方法はないものか、という思いを抱くようになった。

数年間の朝鮮戦争ののち、私はマジソンはウィスコンシン大学の大学院に籍をおき、機械工学の修士号に加え、学際間の哲学博士号を得たが、この学際間博士課程は私に広い範囲での勉強を可能にしてくれた。人生のこの段階にあって、私は工学以外にもいろいろと理解せねばという必要を痛感していた。経済学、労働法、政治学、心理学、哲学、などの諸分野に手を拡げ、これらの分野と工学という私の専門分野とをどうつなげるかを工夫発明することがあった。

私は、マジソン在のウィスコンシン大学、コロンバスのオ

a B-29 gunnery school poised to join one of General Curtis LeMay's B-29 crews in the incineration of Japanese cities, had the war continued.

After the war, as a veteran I was financially assisted through a mechanical engineering education at the University of Minnesota by the GI Bill.[5] I received a bachelor's degree in mechanical engineering from the University of Minnesota in June, 1950, and a Reserve Officer Training Corps commission as a second lieutenant in the US Air Force. A few days after graduation, the Korean War began and I was soon involuntarily recalled to active duty. Still holding those childhood urges to fly, I subsequently volunteered to enter pilot training and found myself, shortly after flight school graduation, assigned as a copilot on a B-29, flying combat bombing missions from Okinawa's Kadena air base to North Korean targets.

My combat experience, though mild, became a seed within me from which a different tree of understanding and concern has grown over the years. Indiscriminate killing and destruction in the dark of night from five miles high, in a 70-ton B-29 deliverer of violence caused me, for the first time, to wonder if there might not be better ways to try and resolve conflicts than by the organized killing and destruction called war.

A few years after Korea, my path led back to graduate school at the University of Wisconsin in Madison, where I earned an engineering masters degree and an interdisciplinary Ph. D. degree that enabled me to study much more broadly. At this stage of my life I felt a strong need to understand more than just engineering. I was able to study some economics, labor law, political science, psychology, and philosophy, and to try and connect these themes to my world of engineering.

I have been an engineering faculty member at the

ハイオ州立大学、アセンスのオハイオ大学などで工学部の教職にあったが、いまではアセンスで名誉教授として老いを養っている。そのほかシアトルのワシントン大学、ワシントンD.C.の工学部生のためのワシントン・インターンシップ、工学ならびに公共政策プロジェクト、愛知県春日井市の中部大学、上海機械工科大学、それにモンタナ州ボズマンのモンタナ州立大学など各所で客員教授をつとめた。

　専門分野でのかかわりや関心領域としては、工学上の品質システム、生産および生産性についての人間的側面、工学ならびに公共政策、設計によるグリーン技術 (GTBD) などがある。GTBDとは、設計のごく最初の段階から資源を節約し汚染を出さぬための仕組みを作りつけた技術を指す。

　私は国家指導者たちが軍事的な玩具をもてあそんではお互いを脅迫しあうゲームに興じる一方で、人々が真に何を必要としているかについては、しばしば知らん顔をしていることに対し、幻滅の度を深めていた。これらの指導者は荒々しい「ミサイル願望」[6]と、強制力や軍事力志向という悲劇的な固定観念に搦めとられ、紛争解決や戦争防止のために、非暴力的非軍事的な方法を追求している人々に対してはとかく侮蔑の目を向けがちである。

　これは一例だが、冷戦が終結した1996年、アメリカ議会と大統領とは、すでに着ぶくれしている国防総省に対し、何百億ドルという追加予算を無理矢理に呑ませた。国防総省が求めてもいない巨額をである。と同時にこの国の指導者どもは、(1) 恵まれない子どもたちのための初期教育計画や、(2) 年配者への健康保健計画、(3) われわれの自然環境をきれいにし、巨大な消費のムダを減らすための予算をカットしようともくろんでいたのである。

University of Wisconsin, Madison; Ohio State University, Columbus; and Ohio University, Athens, where I am presently a retired emeritus professor. Visiting faculty opportunities have been mine at the University of Washington, Seattle (Washington, DC—Washington Internship for Students of Engineering, Engineering and Public Policy Project); Chubu University, Kasugai, Japan; Shanghai Institute of Mechanical Engineering, Shanghai, China; and Montana State University, Bozeman, Montana.

Professional involvements and interests include engineering quality systems, the human face of production and productivity, engineering and public policy, and green technology by design (GTBD). By GTBD I mean resource conserving and non-polluting technology designed that way from the very beginning of the engineering design process.

Over the years I have grown increasingly disillusioned with the way leaders of nations threaten each other and play games with their military toys, while often ignoring the real needs of people. These leaders, afflicted with masculine "missile envy"[6] and a tragic mind-set preference for violence and military force, generally look with disdain on those who seek non-violent, non-military means of conflict resolution and war-and-violence prevention.

For example, with the Cold War ended, in 1996 the US Congress and the president stuffed several additional billions of dollars down the throat of an already bloated Department of Defense—money that department had not even requested. At the same time our leaders sought to (1) cut funding for an early education program for disadvantaged children, (2) cut healthcare for the elderly, and (3) cut efforts to clean up our environment and reduce our enormously wasteful consumption.

1982年、1つにはレーガン政権の軍拡競争の促進への怒り
を静め、心理的な鬱状態を乗り越えるためもあって、私はオ
ハイオ州の第10選挙区から民主党の連邦下院議員の予備選挙
に立候補した。私の選挙綱領は、アメリカの再軍事化に抗し
て、平和と公正の実現をうたっていた。有権者はその訴えに
さほど共鳴してはくれず、落選してしまった。

　私はこの慕わしい母なる地球の市民として、豊かな国々の
貪欲でやみくもな過大消費、生態系や動植物の繁殖自生地の
破壊について、幻滅や懸念の度を深めていった。それはしば
しば軍事中心主義や戦争という暴力と道づれで、豊かな国々
の貧しい国々への資源依存度は高まる一方である。

　1981年、春日井市の中部大学での客員教授職の就任に備え、
私と妻とはオハイオ大学で日本史と日本文化とのクラスに出
て、はじめて日本の平和憲法と第9条の戦争放棄について知
り、深い感銘を受けた。それから10年後、湾岸戦争のみぎり、
私はふたたび憲法9条について思いを致し、新国際秩序――
ブッシュ大統領がしばしば言及していた――にとっての理想
的な基礎はこれだと考えたことであった。

第9条の会の創設

　1991年の3月のなかごろ、アメリカの「石油資源」湾岸戦
争が終わってまもなく、私は考え方を同じくするオハイオ州
アセンスのユニテヤリアン教会の仲間たちと力を合わせ、第
9条の会 (A9S) を発足させた。すべての国の憲法に、日本国
憲法の9条に盛られた諸原則を採択させる、という長期的な

In 1982, in part to overcome anger and a sense of psychological depression caused by the Reagan administration's acceleration of the arms race, I ran in the Democratic Party primary for election to the Ohio 10th District seat in the US House of Representatives. I campaigned on a peace and justice platform in opposition to this renewed militarization of America. The voters were not too receptive to my message. I lost the election.

I am a citizen of our dear planet, Mother Earth, who has become disillusioned and concerned with the mindless greed-driven over-consumption and entropic destruction of habitat and ecosystems by the rich nations, often accompanied by militarism and the violence of war as the rich grow evermore resource dependent on the poorer nations.

In preparation for a visiting professorship at Chubu University in Kasugai City, Japan, in 1981, my wife and I took a course at Ohio University on Japanese history and culture and, for the first time, learned of and were deeply impressed with Japan's Peace Constitution and its eloquent war renouncing Article 9. Ten years later, when the USA fought the Persian Gulf war, I again thought of Article 9 as an ideal basis for the "new world order" to which President George Bush so frequently referred.

Founding of the Article 9 Society

In mid March, 1991, shortly after America's Persian Gulf "oil resource" war, with the encouragement of like-minded persons in our Unitarian Fellowship in Athens, Ohio, I founded The Article 9 Society (A9S), an organization dedicated to the long-term goal of having all nations adopt in their constitu-

目標の達成を目指す組織としてである。昔ながらの戦争への惑溺から自らを解き放つことがいかに容易でないかを認識し、A9Sの長期的な目標に連なる短期的なそれとして以下の数点を定めた。

(1) 日本国民による、国の内外における9条を腐食させ放棄させようという圧力に抗し、憲法9条の真髄を賦活させたいという希望を力づけ助勢していく。

(2) ドイツ国民による紛争解決にあたり、軍事力の行使をいましめた第2次大戦以降の憲法上の制約を維持したいとする希望を力づけ助勢していく。

(3) 日本やドイツの軍事力の行使を禁じた憲法上の制約は、21世紀以降の世界にとって前向きで望ましいモデルであり、国際紛争や戦争防止にとっての非暴力的な解決案として他国も模倣してしかるべきモデルである、という考え方を力づけ助勢していく。

(4) これまた将来に向けてのモデルとして、コスタリカやスイスのように、軍事力の行使を国策として禁じながらもちゃんと生き抜いてきた国々の憲法や慣行の検討を力づけ助勢していく。

(5) すべての国や国連が戦争防止や非暴力的な紛争解決の数多い可能性を洗い出すための啓蒙教育やその実施のためにしかるべき支出を真剣に考慮するよう、力づけ助勢していく。

　第9条の会が湾岸戦争の直後に生まれたのは、希望と絶望との綯い交ぜの中からであった。一縷の希望は東欧やソ連、それに南アフリカで起きていた、信じがたいほどの変革が、

tions the principles expressed in Article 9 of the Japanese Constitution. Recognizing the difficulty in weaning ourselves from the age-old addiction to war, A9S's shorter term goals leading to the long term are:

1. To encourage and support the Japanese people in their desire to restore the integrity to Article 9 of their Constitution in the face of increasing internal and international pressure to erode and abandon it.

2. To encourage and support the German people in their desire to retain their post WW-II constitutional prohibitions against the use of military force in dispute resolution.

3. To encourage and support the idea that Japanese and German constitutional prohibitions against the use of military force should be viewed as positive and desirable models for the 21st century and beyond—models for non-violent international conflict resolution and war prevention, to be emulated by other nations.

4. To encourage and support, also as models for the future, exploration of the constitutions and practices of nations such as Costa Rica, Switzerland and others that have successfully survived without the use of military force as an instrument of governmental policy.

5. To encourage and support efforts by all nations and the United Nations to begin to seriously allocate resources for education in and implementation of the endless possibilities for war prevention and non-violent means of conflict resolution.

The Article 9 Society was born just after the end of the Persian Gulf war, out of a mixture of hope and hopelessness. Threads of hope came from the almost unbelievable transfor-

予想だにできなかった程の少ない暴力で成就しつつあったことに由来した。ミハイル・ゴルバチョフのような世界的な政治指導者が、45年にものぼる冷戦分裂症状とその浪費とを見抜き、こんなナンセンスはもうこれで手じまいに、と断固主張していた。この種のリーダーシップはアメリカからは出てこなかったのだろうか。不幸なことに当時のわが国の指導者連は、「貪欲は偉大だ」などとのたまい、スターウォー技術で宇宙空間を軍事化せねば、などと仰せられていたのである。

他方、絶望はアメリカによる一連の軍事的暴力とのかかわりに発していた。(1) 1991年の湾岸石油資源戦争でイラク人民はハイテクによる大量殺りくを受け、(2) かつてCIAの麻薬販売担当だったマニュエル・ノリエガを追っての1989年のパナマへの侵攻、(3) 1980年代のレーガン時代におけるニカラグア革命への破壊工作、(4) 300万人以上のベトナム人と6万人のアメリカ兵士が、アメリカ指導者の不遜と愚かしさの故に命を落としたベトナムでの惨禍、などがこれであった。25年の後になって、当時の国防長官でベトナム戦争の創始者の1人であったロバート・マクナマラがついにその愚かしさと没義道性とを認めたのは、多少われわれを勇気づけた。[7]

だれしもサダム・フセインの徒を好みはしない。だがアメリカが50万人もの将兵を湾岸地帯に送りこんだのは、決してあの地域の前近代的な封建国家に民主主義をもたらそうとしてではなかった。われわれがあの地域に赴いた主たる理由は、石油、のひとことに尽きる。共和党の右派との間にイメージ上の問題をかかえていたブッシュ大統領は、さっさと小戦争を片付けることで彼の「男らしさ」を示す必要にせまられていたのである。しばらくの間すべては彼の思い通りに運び、湾岸戦争後、彼の支持率は一気に跳ね上がった。でもアメリカ人が自分たちの日常生活という現実に立ち戻るや否や、落ちこむのも速かったのである。

mations taking place in Eastern Europe, the USSR, and in South Africa—with far less violence than could ever have been anticipated. Hope came with world statesman Mikail Gorbachev, who rose to the occasion, recognized the paranoid sickness and waste of the 45-year Cold War standoff and said enough of this nonsense. Would that this kind of leadership had come from America. Unfortunately, at that time our leaders were telling us that "greed is great," and that we needed to militarize space with "star wars" technology.

Hopelessness came from a litany of recent unfortunate American involvements with military violence: (1) the 1991 Persian Gulf oil resource war "high-tech" slaughter of Iraqi people; (2) our 1989 Panama invasion in pursuit of our former CIA drug dealing employee, Manuel Noreiga; (3) the 1980's Reagan years of subversion of the Nicaraguan revolution; and (4) our Vietnam disaster in which three or more million Vietnamese people and sixty thousand American soldiers died because of our leaders' hubris and folly. It is slightly encouraging that twenty-five years later, Robert McNamara, former Secretary of Defense and one of the architects of the Vietnam war, finally admitted to its folly and immorality.[7]

No one cares for the likes of Saddam Hussein, but America did not send 500,000 soldiers to the Persian Gulf to restore democracy to that region of monarchical fiefdoms. Our primary reason for being there was simply "oil." President Bush, who had an image problem with the right-wing of his party, also needed to demonstrate his machismo with a fast little war. It worked, for a while. After the war Bush's popularity in polls rose to very high levels but dropped quickly as Americans got back to the reality of their own lives.

無差別テロをおこなうゲリラが
台頭していたころのペルー。

Peru when indiscriminate ter-
rorism was rampant.

石油資源戦争

　なぜ私が湾岸戦争のことを「石油資源戦争」と呼ぶのかその理由を説明したい。

　われわれは資源の払底が諸国家が戦争に従事する理由の1つであることを知っている。われわれはまた1973年の中東石油危機の際に、アメリカ人が石油ガブ呑みの大型車への給油のために、長い行列を作ることを好まぬことを知った。自分たちの処女石油資源のほとんどを使いつくしてしまったわれわれアメリカ人は、いまや石油消費量の50％以上を輸入に仰いでいる。1990年の9月半ば、われらが被保護者たるサダム・フセインがクウェートに侵攻して6週間後に、アメリカ上院はS1224という法案を廃案にした。

　この法案がもし通っていたとしたら、アメリカで製造販売されるすべての自動車は、2001年までにリッターあたり17キロの燃費効率をもたなければならなかった。それは優に今日の技術的な能力の範囲内にある。

　懸念する科学者連盟は、もしもこの種のグリーン・テクノロジーを奨励していたとすれば、紀元2005年までにわれわれアメリカ人は、クウェートの年間全石油産出量の、優に2倍を上まわる節約を、毎年、ずうっと将来にわたってなしとげることができる、と試算した。われわれは自分たちの身のまわりを整頓し、エネルギー浪費のムダを省くことで、自国の長期的な利益をはかるか、さもなければ軍事力に物をいわせることで、湾岸地域における「自分たちの」石油供給を防衛するか、いずれかの選択の余地を有していたのである。不幸なことながら、われわれが選んだのは、後者の選択だった。

　ブッシュ大統領は湾岸戦争のさなか「新しい世界秩序」を口にした。その通り、と私も思った。でもお互いが必要としている新世界秩序とは、湾岸で示されたような軍事中心主義の上に立つ暴力のそれではなかった。われわれが必要としているのは、日本国憲法の戦争放棄の諸原則をお手本にしたそ

An Oil Resource War

Let me explain why I call the Persian Gulf War an "oil resource" war.

We know that resource scarcity is one of the reasons why nations engage in war. We also found in the 1973 Middle East oil embargo that Americans do not like to have to wait in queues to refuel their gas-guzzling automobiles. Having wastefully consumed much of our own virgin oil resources, we in the United States now import over 50 percent of the oil that we consume. In mid September, 1990, six weeks after our protégé, Saddam Hussein, invaded Kuwait, our US Senate rejected S-1224, a bill that would have required automobiles manufactured and sold in America to have 40 miles-per-gallon (17 kilometers-per-liter) fleet average fuel economy by the year 2001. This is well within the realm of contemporary engineering capability.

The Union of Concerned Scientists calculated that had we encouraged this kind of green technology by design, by the year 2005 we in America would have been saving more than double the entire Kuwaiti annual oil production, every year on into the future. We had a choice of protecting our long term interests by (1) cleaning up our own house and becoming a less energy wasteful nation or (2) using our military force to protect "our" oil supply in the Gulf. Unfortunately, we chose the latter.

President Bush, during the Gulf War, spoke of "A New World Order." It occurred to me that indeed we do need a new world order, but not the militaristic one of violence demonstrated in the Gulf. The new world order we need is one modeled on the war-renouncing principles in Article 9

れだった。憲法9条は戦争防止を目指し国際的な紛争解決に
非軍事的非暴力的な接近をはかるという意味合いをもってい
る。かくしてわれわれの第9条の会は誕生したのであった。

註釈

1. エドワード・C・レイサム（編）『ロバート・フロスト詩集』1969年
   ニューヨーク、ホルト・ラインハート・ウインストン刊。

2. 番場信也、J・ハウズ（共著）「田畑忍：平和憲法の護り手」『日本にお
   ける平和主義：キリスト教と社会主義の伝統』231ページ所収。1978年　京
   都、ミネルヴァ書房刊。

3. ジョン・F・ハッチェソン『慈善の旗手：戦争と赤十字の誕生』前出
   マンは軍事中心主義を「戦争と戦争準備をもって自然で望ましい社会活
   動、とみなす考え方や一連の組織機構」と定義している。

4. ノエル・ペリン『銃を捨てた日本：日本の刀への回帰　1543年〜1879年』
   1979年　ボストン、デビッド・R・ゴッディーン出版刊。日本語版は紀
   伊國屋書店出版部より刊行。川勝平太訳。

5. この法律は連邦議会によって第2次大戦の参戦者を、戦時から平和時へ
   の転換期にあって、大学進学のために経済的な援助を与えることを目的
   として作られた。この法律はまた、元兵士を数年間、労働市場から隔離
   させる、という目的をも果たした。
   　　自分の人生のこの時期を思い出すごとに私の脳裏をよぎるのは、比較
   的豊かな国の政府がその国民という最大の「資源」への投資を促すにあ
   たって、戦争に俟たねばならないのだろうかという疑問だった。この種
   の投資をそれから利益を得ることのできるすべての人々を対象に実行す
   ることこそ、いずれの人々や政府にとってもその最大の利益に合致する
   に決まっているのに、と思われるのだった。受給対象を軍務経験者だけ
   に限定すべきではない。

6. オーストラリアの小児科医で「社会的責任のための医師団」、という組
   織の創設者たるヘレン・カルディコット女史は、しばしば「ミサイル願
   望」という言葉を用い、ペニスさながらのミサイルが他国の諸都市を狙
   っている姿を、男性のペニス願望のあらわれとして比喩的かつ創造的に
   表現した。なおこの組織は米ソ間の核兵器およびミサイル競争の現状に
   反対する医師の集団である。

7. ロバート・S・マクナマラ『ベトナムの悲劇と教訓』1995年　ニュー
   ヨーク・タイムズブックス刊。

of the Japanese Constitution, which imply that we use war prevention, and non-military, non-violent approaches to international conflict resolution. Thus was born our Article 9 Society.

NOTES

1. Lathem, Edward C. (ed.), *The Poetry of Robert Frost*, New York: Holt, Rinehart and Winston, 1969.

2. Bamba, N. and Howes, J., "Tabata Shinobu: Defender of the Peace Constitution," in *Pacifism in Japan: The Christian and Socialist Tradition*. Kyoto, Japan: The Minerva Press, 1978, p. 231.

3. Hutchinson, John F., *Champions of Charity: War and the Rise of the Red Cross*. Westview Press, 1996, p. 6. Mann defines militarism as "… an attitude and a set of institutions which regard war and the preparation for war as a normal and desirable social activity."

4. Perrin, Noel, *Giving Up the Gun: Japan's Reversion to the Sword, 1543–1879*. Boston: David R. Godine Publisher, Inc., 1979.

5. This was a law enacted by the US Congress to assist World War II veterans in the transition from war to peace by enabling them to go to college with government financial support. This law also served the purpose of keeping ex-soldiers out of the labor force for a few years. As I reflect on this period of my life I always find a question coming to mind. Why should it take a war to stimulate a government of a relatively affluent society to make this kind of educational investment in its greatest resource, its people? It occurs to me that this kind of investment in all people who can benefit from it would without doubt be in the best interests of all people and governments everywhere. It should not be confined to only those who have had military service.

6. Helen Caldicott, an Australian pediatrician and founder of Physicians for Social Responsibility, a group of medical doctors in opposition to the sickness of the nuclear arms and missile race between the USA and the USSR, often used the words "missile envy" to creatively and metaphorically describe these erect penislike missiles pointing at each others cities as a manifestation of masculine penis envy.

7. McNamara, Robert S., *In Retrospect: The Tragedy and Lessons of Vietnam*. New York: Times Books, 1995.

バナナ畑につくられた銃の密造工場。どんな材料からでも銃をつくることができる、と彼らはいう。（フィリピン、ミンダナオ島）

Illegal weapons are being put together in the middle of a banana field. They can made a gun out of any material whatsoever, they claim. (Mindanao, Philippines)

憲法9条に関する対論
THE GREAT DEBATE
ON ARTICLE 9

彼らはその剣を鋤に
その槍を鎌に打ち直し
国は国に向かって剣を上げず、
戦いのことを、二度と学ばない

旧約聖書イザヤ書2・4

　経済超大国としての日本が国際問題における自国のもつ機会や責任、それに役割をはっきりさせようとするにあたり、憲法9条にまつわる盛んな討論がおこりつつある。

　憲法9条を変え、「普通の国」としての日本が国際問題での責任を果たすことができるようにしなければ、と主張する向きもある。他方、第9条は現状のままで差しつかえないのに、この半世紀の間にその原則がすっかり侵食されてしまっている以上、その真髄を取り戻すための行動が必要、と説く向きもある。

*... they shall beat their swords into plowshares,
and their spears into pruning hooks:
nation shall not lift up sword against nation,
neither shall they learn war any more.*

Isaiah 2: 4

As Japan seeks to clarify and understand her opportunities, responsibilities, and role in international affairs as an economic superpower, a significant dialogue and debate on Article 9 is taking place. Some argue that Article 9 should be changed so as to make it easier for Japan to assume responsibilities in world affairs as a so-called normal nation. Others feel that Article 9 is OK as it is, but that its principles have been seriously eroded in the half century since it was written, and that actions must be taken to restore its integrity.

私どものように現行のままの第9条に潜む英知に心惹かれている者にとっては、この点について日本はもちろん、全世界においても自由闊達な論議が行われさえすれば、望むらくはその真理に気づく人が増えるに決まっている、と映る。[1]気づきさえすれば、第9条のもつ戦争放棄条項は、新時代における国際関係での礎石の雄の1つとして、真理としての魅力を輝かすにちがいない。

　この討論において問題点がどこにあるかをあいまいにしようと企てる人々もいる。第9条の精神への回帰を唱えてきた1人として、私はこの討論は、史上はじめて経済的に強力な存在となった日本が、国際関係における戦争の行使をその憲法で法的に禁止している、という現実をめぐって起きているものとみなしている。国家主権の一部の棚上げたる戦争放棄など、全世界の政治指導者——日本のそれも含まれる——にとっては、神経を逆撫でされるような、けしからぬ考え方なのである。彼らにしてみれば、法の支配のもと、非暴力非軍事的な紛争解決方法などが国の内外で受容可能な政府の行動様式になりうるとは、考えられもしない奇矯きわまりない話なのだ。だからこそ憲法9条のもつ常軌を逸した趣旨が昔ながらの軍事中心主義的なやり方の前に立ちはだかったりせぬよう、いまのうちに息の根を止めておこうという強い気持ちが存するのである。

　本章では、この憲法9条論議のごく一部を吟味し、第9条の精神を賦活化するために内外から激励を送ることがいかに必要であるかを論じ、新しい時代に向かうにあたり、日本が世界に先駆けて「良心的参戦拒否国家」としての道を開き、軍事力によってではなく、非暴力の代替奉仕活動を通じて世界平和と公正とに寄与していくことの重要性を取り上げていく。

　この「良心的参戦拒否国家」という概念については、本章の後段でさらに論ずることにする。

Those of us who are persuaded by the wisdom of Article 9 as it is feel confident that free and unfettered discussion of Article 9 in Japan and hopefully around the world can but lead to a discovery of its truth by more people.[1] Once discovered, we believe that Article 9's renunciation of war will appeal as a truth that should be one of the major foundation stones of international relations in the new millennium.

Some people try to cloud the issues in this debate. As an advocate for the restoration of Article 9's integrity, it is my assessment that the core of this debate centers on the reality that, for the first time in history, there exists an economically powerful nation, Japan, with a legal prohibition in its constitution against the use of war in international relations. This renunciation of war, a relinquishment of some state sovereignty, is unnerving and a subversive idea to governmental leaders the world over, Japan included. Leaders find it difficult to imagine a world, under a rule of law, in which non-violent and non-military means for conflict resolution are acceptable modes of international and domestic governmental behavior. Therefore, there is a strong desire to destroy this Article 9 before its aberrant message can grow to the point that it might harm the age-old militarist mode of operations.

This chapter will explore a small portion of this Article 9 debate, argue the need for domestic and international encouragement for Japan to restore the integrity of its Article 9, and for Japan to lead the way into the third millennium demonstrating a new model as the world's pioneer and foremost "Conscientious Objector nation," which makes its contribution for world peace and justice not with military force, but rather with non-violent alternative service. The concept of a Conscientious Objector nation will be dealt with later in this chapter.

第9条を書き入れたのはだれ

　第9条を執筆したのは日本人ではなかった、従ってそれを真に日本のものとするためには、書き改めることが必要、と説く向きがある。もしも第9条が日本独特のルーツを欠き、当時の連合軍総司令官たるダグラス・マッカーサー元帥とその幕僚の手になる代物で、1946年、戦いに敗れた日本人に無理矢理に押しつけたものであるとするなら、この改訂必要論も、日本人、とくに戦後生まれで第2次大戦なるものがそれほどの恐怖であり得たかについて生の記憶をもっていない若い層にとっては、ある種の魅力があろう。だが憲法9条の中心的な着想は、当時の幣原喜重郎総理の個人史の中にその起源を有しているように思われる。[2] 何人かの研究者、それにマッカーサー元帥自身が、第9条の本質部分は同総理の提案になることを示唆している。

　1955年、アメリカの在郷軍人グループへの講演の中でマッカーサーは戦争準備をやめる必要と、第2次大戦中に日本人が体験したハイテク大量殺戮について語ったが、その席上、幣原氏との出会いを次のように明かした。「日本の老宰相たる幣原氏が自分のところにやって来て、日本を救うためには、国際的な手段としての戦争を廃絶しなければならない、と訴えたものだった。自分が賛意を表すると、彼は『私たちは世間知らずの夢想家として世界の物笑いになるでしょう。でも100年後には、予言者と呼ばれることでしょう』と言葉を継ぐのだった。」[3,4]

　幣原氏の歩んだ軌跡が、第9条のような条項を挿入するよう主張したことと平仄があっていることを示す新しい証拠が出ている。国際関係への日本の貢献史のアンバランスを正すべく、ドイツの学者クラウス・シュリクトマンは幣原首相の生涯と彼が生きた時代について綿密な研究を行い、幣原が平和問題に関して長年にわたる卓越した閲歴をもつことを跡づけた。[5] 幣原の平和問題へのかかわりは、1899年の昔、ヘーグでの第1回平和会議に若手外交官として参列したことに端を

Authorship of Article 9

Some argue that Article 9 was not written by Japanese people and therefore it should be rewritten and revised so as to make it truly Japan's. If one assumes that Article 9 had no indigenous origins and that it was the creation of the Supreme Commander Allied Powers, General Douglas MacArthur, and his staff who forced it upon a defeated Japan in 1946, this revision argument might have some appeal, especially for those born after the war with no living memory of the terror that was World War II. It appears, however, that the core idea for Article 9 has its roots in the life path of then Prime Minister Kijūrō Shidehara.[2] Various scholars and Douglas MacArthur himself tell us that Shidehara suggested that the essence of Article 9 be a part of the new constitution.

Speaking to an American veteran's group in 1955 about the need to stop making war and the Japanese people's World War II experience of modern high-technology mass annihilation, MacArthur said that "their wise old Prime Minister, Shidehara, came to him and urged that to save themselves they should abolish war as an international instrument. When he agreed, Shidehara turned to him and said, 'The world will laugh and mock us as impractical visionaries, but a hundred years from now we will be called prophets.'"[3, 4]

There is new evidence that Shidehara's path in life was consistent with his advocacy for an Article 9 type clause in Japan's new constitution. Seeking to bring balance into the history of Japan's contribution to international relations, German scholar Klaus Schlictmann has studied extensively the life and times of Prime Minister Shidehara.[5] He found that Shidehara had a long and distinguished track record of involvement with peace issues starting with his participation

発し、1921〜22年のワシントン海軍軍縮会議では日本の首席代表を務めるに至る。第1次大戦後には、戦争廃絶のためのさまざまな国際的な努力に参画、駐米大使としてこれらの動きの主役のだれかれと親しい交わりをもった。その中には、ウッドロー・ウィルソン米大統領やフランク・B・ケロッグ米国務長官らが含まれている。ケロッグ長官はフランスのアリスティード・ブリアン外相とともに1928年8月27日、いわゆるパリ平和協定を結んだが、これには憲法9条もかくやの戦争放棄条項が含まれている。

　幣原氏の平和への数多くのかかわりや、マッカーサーをはじめとする多くの人々の証言のおかげで、憲法9条の中味には「日本製」の部分が少なからずあることを私は確信するに至った。第9条は日本人の魂の奥底からの叫びであった。日本人は第2次大戦の軍国主義者を通じ、「剣によって立つものは剣によって滅ぶ」[6]という聖句の正しさを生々しく身につけていたからである。戦後生まれの日本人の中にはこの教訓が理解できぬ者があるかも知れない。私としては、第9条は日本のものでないから改訂されてしかるべきである、とする議論には首肯しがたいものを覚えるのである。

　いずれにせよ、第9条の着想を最初に出したのがだれだったか、という点はどうでもよい。大切なのは憲法9条と憲法前文とは、戦争のもつ人もなげな野蛮さや暴力性にピリオドを、という全人類の切実な叫びの重要かつ不可欠な表現である、という事実である。いわゆる「普通の国」とやらを目指して9条改訂を企てたりする代わりに、主権者としての日本国民が第9条の真髄をすべての側面において賦活させるよう声を上げることを望みたい。

as a young Japanese career diplomat at the 1899 First Peace Conference at the Hague, and through his role as Japan's chief negotiator at the 1921–22 Washington Naval Disarmament Conference. After World War I Shidehara was a participant in international efforts to abolish war, and as the Japanese ambassador in Washington, he was well acquainted with many of the main actors in this movement. These people included American President Woodrow Wilson and US Secretary of State Frank B. Kellogg, who along with France's Minister of Foreign Affairs, Aristide Briand, authored the August 27, 1928, Paris Peace Pact treaty that renounced war much like Article 9 does.

The long list of Shidehara's peace involvements and the testimony of many people, including General MacArthur, persuades me that Article 9 has a substantial "made in Japan" content. It came from the heart and soul of Japan, a nation that graphically learned from its World War II militarists the truth of the Biblical passage, "They that liveth by the sword shall also perish by the sword."[6] Some Japanese born after the war may not understand this lesson. I am not persuaded by those who claim that since Article 9 is not Japan's it must be revised.

In any event, the issue of whose idea it was is irrelevant. Article 9 and the Constitution's Preamble are essential and important expressions of humanity's cry for an end to the arrogant brutality and violence of war. Rather than revise Article 9 so as to permit Japan to be a so-called normal nation, it is imperative that sovereign Japanese people insist on the restoration of its integrity in all dimensions.

日本は仲間はずれ国家ではない

　憲法9条の戦争放棄条項にしばられてきたために、日本は他の大国や国連自身から村八分にされ尊敬されないある種の「仲間はずれ国家」になってしまった、という主張がある。[7] ということは、尊敬をかち得るためには、すべからく第9条を変え、自衛隊が国連などの軍事活動に世界中で自由に参加できるように仕向けなければならぬ、ということを意味する。軍事的な兄貴分たるアメリカと手をたずさえて、というわけだ。

　著名な政治家たる小沢一郎は、日本は「普通の国」にならねばならぬ、とする。彼のいう「普通の国」とは国際社会にあって当然とされるような責任を喜んで背負う国のことである。[8] 小沢が憲法9条について懸念を抱いていることは、日本のように世界の平和と安定とに大きく依拠している国が、その国際貢献の中から安全保障の役割だけを外すとは、と自問自答している点に明らかに見てとれる。

　これらの問題点に関する国内の論争で、読売新聞の論調は「仲間はずれ国家」「普通の国」という二分法を反映しているが、こういう捉え方自体の背後にはこの問題への憲法9条の「寄与」が見え隠れしている。[9] 同紙は憲法改正案を発表しているが、その目標の1つは「一国平和主義」的な考え方をとり除くことにあり、そうすることで日本にその国際的な責任をよりよく果たさせよう、とする点にある。読売憲法草案は自衛力をもつことの合憲性と日本が国際的責任を果たす必要性とを明確にうたいこむことで、この目的を達成しようというのである。

　新しい一千年期への歴史的な転換期にあって何が必要とされるかといえば、いざの際にはポケットの中に秘めた軍事的なこぶしに物をいわせる式の「普通の国」をあと1つ増やすことではない。それではいままでの二千年間とかわらない。

Japan Not an "Outcast Nation"

Some argue that because Japan has been constrained by Article 9's renunciation of war, it has become a kind of "outcast nation," disrespected by other world powers and the United Nations.[7] This argument suggests that in order to earn respect, Japan must revise Article 9 so as to permit its Self-Defense Forces (SDF) to freely participate in United Nations and other military activities around the globe along with its military big brother, the USA.

Well-known Japanese politician Ichiro Ozawa feels that Japan must become a "normal nation," which he defines as one that willingly shoulders those responsibilities regarded as natural in the international community.[8] His concern with Article 9 is reflected when he asks how can a Japan which so depends on world peace and stability seek to exclude a security role from its international contribution?

In the Japanese dialogue on these issues, the *Daily Yomiuri* newspaper reflects the "outcast nation" and "normal nation" view of things and Article 9's contribution to this perceived problem for Japan.[9] The *Yomiuri* outlines one of the principal goals of its proposed draft revision of the Constitution as eliminating the self-centered "one country pacifism, one country prosperity" mode of thinking so that Japan may better fulfill its international responsibilities. This, their proposed constitution would accomplish by stipulating in clear terms the constitutionality of possessing self-defense capabilities and the need for Japan to fulfill its international responsibilities.

What is needed at this historic time of transition to the third millennium is not another "normal nation" that operates, like all the others have over the past millennia, with a military fist in its pocket of last resort. What the world so

いまの世界が喘ぐように求めているのは、「創造的に普通ではない国」、つまりは従来の軍事力という規範から離れて、非暴力非軍事という斬新きわまりない路線をえらび、従来型との差異においてユニークな国家運営のあり方を見せてくれる国、なのである。この路線こそが歴史が日本に対し懇請している点であり、この地球というホシに住むお互いすべてにとって憲法9条が残す希望に充ちた遺産なのである。

　ここで大切な問いかけは、主権者としての日本国民が果たして自国政府にこの約束を果たさせるだけの力とエネルギーと展望とを動員しうるか否か、という点であろう。

　それにしても、日本の指導者にとって、憲法9条の普遍的な意義と重要性とを認識することが、なぜこんなにも難しいのだろうか。それも第9条が日本にとってのみならず、新しい一千年期を迎えるにあたり、すべての国家と国連にとっての手本として、また生き残りのための指針として、ユニークな潜在性をもっているというのに、である。

　堂々と胸を張り、第9条の精神に見合った形でその責任を果たしていく上で世界規模でのリーダーシップを発揮していくことが、なぜそんなにも難しいのだろうか。

　これらの問いに対する答えは恐らくは歴史を通じて培われた軍事中心主義のもつ魔性にこそ存在するのであろう。すなわち戦争とそのための準備とは普通の望ましい社会活動である、とする考え方に長くなじんできたからであろう。この病弊から癒されることは、日本のみならずほとんどの国家指導者にとって極めてむずかしい。だからこそ、戦争という名の不合理そのものの残虐にピリオドを打ち、非暴力手段こそが第3千年期においては常態たるべきであるという主張を組織し、それを集団的に政府に迫っていく責任は、むしろ一般国民の側にこそ存するのである。

desperately needs is a "Creatively Abnormal Nation"—one that deviates from this past norm of military force, one that demonstrates a new and uniquely different path of non-violent and non-military modes of operation. This is history's pleading call to Japan. This is Article 9's hopeful legacy for all of us on planet Earth. The significant question is: Will the sovereign Japanese people be able to muster the strength, energy and vision to move their government to deliver on this promise?

Why is it so difficult for many Japanese leaders to recognize the universal significance and importance of Article 9, not only for their own nation, but significantly for its unique potential as a model and survival guide for all nations and the United Nations in the new millennium? Why do they feel that they must apologize for this profound and unique set of seventy-three honorable words of wisdom in their constitution? Why is it so difficult for them to stand tall and with pride demonstrate truly world-class international leadership for fulfilling Japan's responsibilities in ways that are consistent with Article 9?

Perhaps the answer to the above questions resides in the addictive power of militarist ideas throughout the course of history—that war and the preparation for war is a normal and desirable social activity. Because it is so difficult for most national leaders, including those in Japan, to cure themselves of this addiction, it must become the people's responsibility to organize and collectively insist that this irrational brutality called war be ended, and that non-violent means become the new norm in the third millennium.

アウシュビッツ強制収容所跡。（ポーランド）
Site of the Auschwitz concentration camp, Poland.

世界規模での文化的規範を形成する

1993年に第9条の会の講演で日本を訪れた折に、私はまず冒頭にロバート・フロストの有名な詩の1節を披露した。

　　二つの道が森の中で別れた
　　私は人があまり通らない方の道を選んだ
　　それが大きなちがいを生んだのだった
　　——通らなかった道——

日本が憲法9条を変更ないしは改訂するようにとの国の内外の圧力にさらされ、世界の尊敬を手にし経済力に見合った責任を果たせるかどうかの狭間に陥っていることに思いを至すにあたり、このフロストの1節を引くことはまことに当を得ている。日本はいまや2つの道のいずれを選ぶか、という大きな選択をせまられている。ほとんどの国が歩んできた、国際関係で軍事力を行使するという失敗に終わった道か、それとも憲法9条の、歩む人とて少ないが道義的な原理原則に基づいた道、をとるかの二者択一である。もし日本が憲法9条の道をとることに成功したら、全人類は「大きなちがいを生んだ」と声を揃えることができよう。

もしも日本があえてこの挑戦に応え、憲法9条の戦争放棄条項を名誉ある勲章として、人通りの少ない道をとるとするならば、日本は世界規模での文化的規範を新たに創り上げる契機たりうる。つまりは国家主権の一部たる交戦権の放棄をその特徴とする国際関係上の新しいパラダイムが、これである。クリストファー・D・ストーンは文化的規範と法との相互関連について述べている。彼によれば、「人はふつう法をすでに広く受け入れられている規範から生まれ、それに権威ある表現を付与する何ものか、と捉えている。だが法の誕生を単に既存の文化的規範の反映とのみ見なすのは、両者間の成りゆきの半面を捉えているにすぎない。逆に法は規範自体

Shaping a Worldwide Cultural Norm

In our 1993 Article 9 Society lecture journey in Japan, I began my talk with a selection from Robert Frost's well known poem, "The Road Not Taken."

> Two roads diverged in a wood, and I—
> I took the one less traveled by,
> And that has made all the difference.

I think that this selection is most appropriate for our reflection on Japan's dilemma in the world as she faces internal and international pressure to change or redefine Article 9 in order to earn respect and fulfill her responsibilities in the world commensurate with her economic power. Japan is faced with a significant choice as to which of two roads to take—the path most traveled upon, the unsuccessful trail of military force in international relations, or the morally principled path, "less traveled by," that is Article 9. If Japan can succeed in taking the Article 9 road, all humanity might be able to say, "and that has made all the difference."

If Japan should rise to the challenge and take this less traveled road with its Article 9 legal injunction against war as its badge of honor, it can be instrumental in shaping a new worldwide cultural norm—a new paradigm for international relations that highlights the renunciation of war as a sovereign right of the nation-state. As Chistopher D. Stone argues in his discussion of the interplay between cultural norms and the law, "One ordinarily thinks of laws as arising out of, and as giving authoritative expression to, norms that already enjoy broad acceptance. ... But the conception of laws as mere reflectors of cultural norms grasps only half the dynamic.

の形成にもかかわっては、その規範が行動の形成者として究極的にどこまで成功するかを決めもする。」[10] 彼のこの主張は、この点で興味ぶかい。

　彼は1950年代、60年代、70年代のアメリカにおける権利確保のための諸運動を例にあげて解説する。黒人の公民権運動、女性自立運動、環境保全運動などがこれである。これらの争点についての法律がひとたび成立すると、こんどはこれらの法律が運動家たちによって一般大衆をさらに啓蒙する手だてとして使われ、大衆の意識や見解を変え、いっときは嘲笑や侮蔑とともにはねつけられ、あまりにも理想論にすぎると相手にされなかったような考え方が、妥当性をもち受容可能な社会規範として認められるようになる。その一例として1920年8月の憲法修正第19条は、婦人参政権を認めたものだが、この修正は男女間の平等という考え方を推し進める上にあずかって力があった。60年代の公民権法案も、白人のアメリカ人に黒人の平等を受け入れさせる上に大きな助けとなった。

　日本は憲法で戦争を禁じた世界で唯一の主要国家である。もしこの条項が、日本が「普通の国」になる上の障害として、何か恥ずかしい存在であるかのようにではなく、日本のリーダーたちによって尊厳と名誉と尊敬とをもって遇せられるならば、憲法9条は他の国々や国連が、紛争解決の上で軍事中心主義を退けるという意味での強力なパラダイムを創り上げることで、新しい文化的規範へと前進することができよう。

日本の自衛隊はすでに第9条を破壊した

　この第9条をめぐる論争において、第9条は日本が従うべきモデルとしてはすでに時代おくれ、とみなす向きがある。す

Laws also contribute to the fashioning of norms on which their success as moulders of conduct will ultimately depend."[10]

To illustrate, he uses examples of the various rights movements in the USA in the 1950s, '60s and '70s,—the black civil rights movement, the women's and the environmental movements, etc. Once laws related to these issues are in place, they then assist advocates in further educating the public. They help to change public consciousness and opinion so that ideas that, at one time, might have been dismissed with ridicule, contempt, or as hopeless idealism come to be accepted as legitimate and acceptable societal norms. For example, the August, 1920, Nineteenth Amendment to the US Constitution giving women the right to vote was helpful in furthering the idea that women and men are equal. The civil rights legislation of the 1960s helped white Americans grow to accept the equality of blacks.

Japan is the only major world power with this law, this legal injunction against war in its constitution. If forcefully promoted by Japanese leaders with a sense of dignity, honor, and respect, rather than being treated as something of which to be ashamed, something that constrains Japan from becoming a so-called normal nation, Article 9 can help other nations and the United Nations move to a new cultural norm by establishing a powerful new paradigm for the resolution of conflict that excludes militarism.

Japan's Self-Defense Forces Have Already Destroyed Article 9

In this great debate some say that it is already too late to hold Article 9 as a model for Japan to follow, because its essence

でにしてその本質は、強大な自衛隊という名の軍隊によって破壊されてしまっているから、というのである。

　私はこの考え方には与しない。私が現役の兵士として参加したかの朝鮮戦争以来、たしかに憲法9条が貶められ空洞化されたのは事実である。でもほとんどの人が気づいていないのは、第2次大戦の終結このかた、主としてこの73語の金言のおかげで、日本以外の土地で日本兵によって殺された人間がただの1人もいない、[11] という点である。アメリカやソ連、それに他の大国と較べて、これは日本人たるもの大いに誇ってよいみごとな実績である。

　憲法9条が次々に侵食されていくのをお手上げだとして、手を拱いている代わりに、われわれは日本国民が憲法に保証された主権者としての権利を行使し、事態の転換をはかり、その理想の顕現に向かって着実な歩みを進めるよう、勇気づけるべきである。日本国民もまた自国政府に対し、これからのすべての日米安保条約の交渉にあたっては、憲法9条という平易にして容易に理解できる言葉の実体が賦活する方向に着実に向かうような形で、力強く名誉ある交渉を行なっていくよう主張すべきである。ごく最近の1996年4月の日米安保交渉は明らかに憲法9条の精神の復活に向かうような交渉内容ではなかった。

人道的援助や救援奉仕活動機関としての軍隊

　日本には、自衛隊は、たとえば1995年の阪神淡路大震災のときのように、非常の際に人道的救援活動に従事することで、少なくともその存在理由の一部は認めることができる、とする論がある。同様の理由づけはアメリカの軍隊や州兵組織についても聞かれる。

has been destroyed by the existence of a very powerful military called the Self-Defense Forces.

I do not agree. It is true that since the Korean War (my war as a combat soldier) Article 9 has been seriously compromised and eroded. Few people realize, however, that for over half a century, since the end of World War II, primarily because of these seventy-three honorable words in Japan's Constitution, no person outside of Japan has been killed by Japanese soldiers.[11] When compared to the USA and the USSR and other world powers, this is a remarkable record of which Japanese people should be proud.

Rather than hopelessly give up and accept this continuous erosion of Article 9, we must encourage Japanese people to exercise their constitutionally derived sovereign power to turn things around and steadily move their nation toward fulfillment of the ideal. Japanese people must insist that their government, in all future Japan-United States Security Agreement negotiations, forcefully and honorably negotiate agreements that steadily move toward a restoration of the integrity of those very plain, simple, and easily understood words of Article 9. The most recent Japan-US Security Agreement, April 1996, is clearly not one that leads toward the restoration of Article 9's integrity.

The Military As a Humanitarian Relief and Rescue Service Institution

Some in Japan argue that the SDF's existence can, in part, be justified by its being there in time of need to provide humanitarian relief and rescue for such natural disasters as the 1995 Kobe area earthquake. Similar justifications are made for the military and the National Guard in America.

戦争や内線が原因で国を追われたり、
住んでいた場所を離れなくてはいけ
なくなった人の数は、世界中で2700
万人に達した。（エチオピア、ソマリ
ア難民キャンプ）

Owing to war and internal conflict,
twenty-seven million people around
the world had to emigrate or abandon
their homes. (Camp for Somalian
refugees in Ethiopia)

国の内外を問わず、天災もしくは人災の際に人道的な救援活動の必要があることは、明白である。だが、この種の不可欠なサービスの提供にあたっては、人道的な救援活動や災害救出活動について専門的な訓練を受け、そのことを主たる任務とする組織に属する若者の手で行われる方が、もっとよいのではないだろうか。

　軍隊の主たる機能とはいくさに勝つことにある。兵士が訓練されているのは相手を殺し、破壊することについてである。軍事訓練であれ軍隊の機能であれ、災害に見舞われ苦しんでいる人々が必要とするものとは全く逆である。

　だから、日本の自衛隊であれどこの国の軍隊であれ、人道的な救援活動を行うに適した組織である、などという論議を受け入れぬようにしようではないか。この手の妄論は、一般市民に軍隊という負担を受け入れさせるための目くらましとして、軍事中心主義とこれら重要な人道的な機能とを同一視せんがために繰り出されることがしばしばである。必要なのは、人道的な災害救援活動を主たる役割とする新組織である。これを人道的救援グループと呼ぶことにしよう。

日米安保取り決め

　この本のほかでも述べたように、第9条のただならぬ侵食過程は、新憲法が制定された直後に早くも始まっていた。この侵食をもたらしたのは、朝鮮半島とベトナムとの熱い戦争で中断したとはいえ引き続く冷戦体制と、アメリカ側の国防上の必要とであった。憲法9条がないがしろにされたのは、日米安保取り決めのせいである。もっとも最近の侵食は1996年4月、日米両国が新しく拡大された条約に署名し、2国間の防衛協力向けの既存のガイドラインの見直しに合意したときである。

Obviously there is a need for humanitarian relief and rescue activity within nations and around the globe in natural and human-made disasters. Would it not be better, however, to provide this kind of essential service with youth who are specifically trained in humanitarian relief and disaster response, and who are members of an organization whose primary function is exactly that?

The primary function of a military is win in a conflict. Soldiers are trained to kill and destroy. Military training and the military function are the very antithesis of what is needed by suffering people afflicted with disaster.

Let us therefore not accept these arguments that the SDF, or the military in any country, is the appropriate institution to carry out humanitarian relief and rescue activities. These arguments are often used to associate militarism with these essential humanitarian functions in order to persuade citizens to accept the burdens of a military. What is needed is a new institution whose primary function is humanitarian relief and disaster assistance. Let us call it a Humanitarian Relief Group.

Japan–United States Security Agreement

As I have pointed out elsewhere in this book, serious erosion of Article 9 began almost as soon as Japan's new constitution was adopted. The Cold War, punctuated with hot wars in Korea and Vietnam, and America's defense needs, has driven this erosion. Japan–US security agreements have been the vehicles by which Article 9 has been compromised. The latest erosion took place in April, 1996, when Japan and the USA signed a new and expanded security agreement and also agreed to review existing guidelines for bilateral defense cooperation.

現行の日本政府の憲法解釈によれば、いわゆる集団自衛権の行使は禁じられている。ということは攻撃を受けた場合なら自衛のために応戦できるが、日本への直接攻撃でない戦争にあっては兵站補給の面その他でアメリカ軍と協同作戦を行うことはできない、とされている。

　この憲法上の制約については最近再解釈が行われ、その結果、訓練や平和維持活動において両国が兵站補給面で協力することはいまや容易となっている。[12]

　1995年に沖縄の少女がアメリカ海兵隊員らによって暴行されたという不幸な事件は、これらの諸問題についての討議を焦点のしぼりこんだものにした。日本の安保についての論議は、(1) 条約の完全な破棄を主張するもの、(2) 新しい条約が結ばれることに憲法を再解釈していけば済むと皮肉な見方をとるもの、(3) 憲法を変えることで、日本が軍隊をもって集団自衛権を行使し、世界規模での国連その他の平和維持活動に安んじて参加できるようにする、という3種類に大別できる。

　アメリカは日本の憲法9条を承認し尊重せねばならない。これからの一切の日米安保論議においては第9条の真意の復活に着実に向かっていくような方向での変化を慫慂していくべきなのである。だが外部からの圧力でも加えられぬ限り、こんなことは考えられそうにない。であるとすれば、日本人自身がこれからのすべての安保取り決め論議で着実かつ断固としてそちらの方向を目指すべきであり、日本の世界平和と公正への貢献は非暴力・非軍事的な戦争防止と紛争解決であるべきである、とする立場をつよく主張してよい。

　憲法9条の全き尊重とは、沖縄や日本の他地域におけるアメリカ軍の段階的削減を含意している。

As the Japanese government presently interprets their constitution, Japan is prohibited from exercising the right of collective self-defense. This means that it can only defend itself if attacked, but not cooperate logistically or otherwise with the USA in any war that is not a direct attack on Japan. Apparently some reinterpretation of this constitutional constraint has recently been arranged so that it is now easier for the two countries to assist each other with logistical support in training and peacekeeping activities.[12]

The unfortunate 1995 Okinawan rape by US soldiers has helped to sharpen the debate on these issues. The security agreement debate in Japan includes (1) those who advocate the complete abrogation of the agreement, (2) those who cynically suggest that the constitution need only be reinterpreted so as to enable it to accommodate each new agreement, and (3) those who wish to change the constitution so as to permit Japan to participate, with military forces, in collective self-defense and in all UN and other peace-keeping activities around the world.

The United States should honor and respect Japan's Article 9 by encouraging changes in all future Japan–US Security Agreement negotiations that steadily move toward the restoration of the integrity of Article 9. Since this is not likely to occur without some pressure, Japanese people themselves must insist that all future Japan–US security agreements steadily and inexorably move in that direction and permit Japan to make its contributions to world peace and justice with non-violent, non-military approaches to conflict resolution and war prevention. Full integrity of Article 9 implies that there be a phased reduction of the US military presence on Okinawa and in the rest of Japan.

良心的参戦拒否国家としての日本は、ヨーロッパの安全保障協力機構ばりのアジア太平洋地域での新しい機構において指導性を発揮することを求められよう。日本が力点をおき貢献すべき分野は協力であり、安全保障のための非暴力的手段にあることは言うまでもない。

　核兵器の惨禍に一度ならず見舞われた、地球上の唯一の国民として日本人は、1980年代初期のニュージーランドのデビッド・ロンギ元首相がそうだったように、アメリカの「核の傘」なるものから自らを解き放つ権利を手に入れている。これはいまでは以前よりずっと容易である。現にアメリカ戦略空軍の前司令官のリー・バトラー退役将軍が、核兵器は全廃されるべきであり、アメリカはその方向に向かって主導権をとるべきである旨を、ついさきごろも世界に向かって発表したほどである。[13] SACというのはアメリカの核兵器の運搬システムである。バトラー将軍も、(1) 冷戦は終結した、(2) 核兵器は本来的に危険で、すこぶる高くつくのに軍事的には非能率で、核戦争とは血ぶくれた荒々しい猛獣のようなもので、その本能と食欲とを理解しているふりこそしてはいるが調教などとてもおぼつかない上に、(3) アメリカの役割の決定的な大きさを思うと、やはりアメリカが核政策や核戦略の抜本的な見直しの先頭を切らないかぎり、ことは始まらない、としている程である。

　この見解表明や結論づけには、全世界の60人ほどの退役将軍や提督が署名賛成している。[14]

　憲法9条の真髄の全面的な復権に自国を向かわせようとするにあたり、日本の皆さんは少なからぬ挑戦に向かいあうことになろう。この転換にあたっては軍事志向のつよい内外の人士からの、この原則路線を掘り崩そうとする大変な圧力に出会うことであろう。
「良心的参戦拒否」路線をスタートさせその路線を維持し、

Perhaps Japan could be encouraged to exercise leadership as a Conscientious Objector nation in a new Asia-Pacific organization somewhat like the Organization for Security and Cooperation in Europe. Japan's emphasis and contribution should be on cooperation and non-violent means for security.

As the only people on Earth to have been afflicted with nuclear holocausts, Japanese people have earned the right to take Japan out from under America's so-called nuclear umbrella, as did former New Zealand Prime Minister David Lange in the early 1980s. This should be easier to do now that the former commander of the US Strategic Air Command, retired General Lee Butler, recently announced to the world that nuclear weapons ought to be reduced to zero, and that the United States ought to take a leadership role in moving toward that end.[13] SAC is America's nuclear weapons delivery system. Butler said that (1) the Cold War is over; (2) that nuclear weapons are inherently dangerous, hugely expensive, and militarily inefficient, and nuclear war is a raging, insatiable beast whose instincts and appetites we pretend to understand but cannot possibly control; and (3) that given its crucial leadership role, it is essential for the United States to undertake as a first order of business a sweeping review of its nuclear policies and strategies. Some sixty other retired admirals and generals from around the world concur in these observations and conclusions.[14]

Japanese people will face significant challenges as they attempt to move Japan toward restoration of the full integrity of Article 9. In this transition there will be much pressure from militaristically oriented persons, both domestically and internationally, to subvert this principled path. Much courage, strength and vision will be demanded of Japanese citizens in

冷戦時代に大量生産された原子力船や原子力潜水艦が、原子炉もはずされないまま捨てられている。（ロシア、ムルマンスク）

The huge number of nuclear-powered ships and submarines build during the Cold War are cast aside without removing the nuclear reactors. (Murmansk, Russia)

普通の国が長い間実践してきた軍事力と戦争との昔ながらの路線に復帰させまいとすれば、日本の市民に多大な勇気と力、それに未来展望とが求められよう。

日本と国連

　国連安保理の常任理事国の数を増やそうという動きが伝えられる。もし常任理事国になれば、国連の平和維持活動に参加する義務が生じ、憲法9条に違反することになる、という理由で反対する声もある。でも私はその立場には与しない。日本は、できるだけ速やかに常任理事国の席を占め、その基本的な道義上法律上の手引きとしての憲法9条を堂々と持ちこみ、良心的参戦拒否国の一員として国連のすべての活動に参加すべきであると私は考える。日本は国連内部でリーダーシップを振るい、平和と安定への国連の貢献は、第9条をはじめとする日本国憲法と完全に合致した非軍事的な性格のものに限られるべきだと、強力に主張すべきである。日本はまた憲法9条の諸原則が国連自体やすべての国々の基礎文書に組み入れられるべく、着実かつ不断に努力していかねばならない。

　世界でもっとも強力な経済大国としての日本は、国連のさまざまな改革にあたっては、主導的な役割を果たしていくべきである。その中でもっとも緊急かつ困難な改革は、安保理事会の改組であり、古ぼけた拒否権という仕組みを現在の5つの常任理事国の手から奪い去ることである。アメリカ、ロシア、英国、フランス、それに中国がこの5ヵ国である。

　「良心的参戦拒否国」の一員としての日本は、国連憲章の第4章、

order to launch and keep their nation on a conscientious objector path and to avoid a reversion to the old familiar path of military force and war so long practiced by normal nations.

Japan and The United Nations

There is talk about increasing the number of permanent members of the UN Security Council. Some argue that Japan should not become a permanent member of the Security Council because to do so would obligate it to participate in UN military peace-keeping operations which would be in violation of Article 9. I disagree with this position. I think that Japan should become a permanent member of the UN Security Council, as soon as possible, and that it proudly bring with it Article 9 as its fundamental moral-legal guide for participation in all UN activities as a Conscientious Objector nation. Japan should provide leadership in the UN and forcefully insist that its UN contributions to peace and security be of a non-military nature that is completely consistent with Article 9 and other parts of its Peace Constitution. Japan should steadily and continuously seek to have Article 9 principles integrated into the foundation documents of all nations and of the UN itself.

As one of the world's most economically powerful nations Japan should provide leadership in the UN for numerous kinds of UN reforms. One of the most difficult and urgent of these would be the reorganization of the Security Council and elimination of the archaic veto power of the present five permanent members, the USA, Russia, the United Kingdom, France and China.

As a CO nation, Japan might well exercise strong leader-

すなわち「紛争の平和的解決」に関する章の発展強化、それに実施の面で強いリーダーシップを振るってしかるべきだろう。

国連の安全保障グループ

　世界の大半の国が法の支配のもとで、軍事力の代わりに、憲法9条的な諸原則を紛争処理に適用するようになるのにはまだまだ時間がかかろう。その長い過渡期の間、日本は常設の国連安全保障グループの創設と運営とに国連内部でリーダーシップをとっていかねばならない。この新組織は、国連の指揮のもとに、暴力や戦争がその醜い鎌首をもたげた問題地域なら世界中のどこであれ時を移さず対応できるような、国際的な警察平和維持機関である。この機関は世界各国からの個人的ボランティアから構成されるべきで、資金面は累進性の国連税によってまかなわれ、地球資源の消費量と生物圏の汚染の度合いに応じて課税されるものとする。とりあえずは1国の国民総生産に応じて課税額が決まるが、よりよい算定方式が見出されればそれに代えられる。

　このUNSG案を組織し運用していくためには、諸国が伝統的な主権の一部を差し出さねばならないが、これは極めてむずかしい、でも手を染めねばならぬことである。

　たとえばアメリカ議会はいやしくもアメリカ軍の兵士たるものが国連の指導官から命令を受領することに頑として反対している。またアメリカには、ボランティアがUNSGに参加することや、それを支えるための税法のあり方についても強い反対が予想される。

　百パーセント、ボランティアから成り、国連の指揮下にお

ship for further development, strengthening and implementation of Chapter VI of the UN Charter, the chapter on "Pacific Settlement of Disputes."

The United Nations Security Group

It will take some time before most of the nations of the world adopt Article 9 type principles and agree to settle disputes under the rule of law rather than with military force. In the lengthy transition period, Japan should provide leadership within the UN for the creation and implementation of a permanent United Nations Security Group (UNSG). This UNSG would be an international police and peace-keeping organization that could rapidly respond, under UN command, to problem areas around the world wherever violence and war show their ugly heads. The UNSG should be composed of individual volunteers from all nations of the world. It should be funded by a progressive UN tax on all nations in proportion to their consumption of Earth's resources and their pollution of the biosphere. A nation's gross national product might be a beginning measure for taxing, until a better one could be found.

In order to organize and implement this proposed UNSG, nations would have to surrender some of their traditional sovereignty—a very difficult thing to achieve, but something that needs to begin. The US Congress, for example, adamantly opposes having any US soldier take orders from UN commanders. There would probably also be strong objection in America to having US volunteers serve in the UNSG as well as to the taxation idea for supporting it.

An all volunteer UNSG commanded by UN officers

かれるということなら、日本の若者も憲法9条に抵触することなしに国連の平和維持活動に加わりえよう。

軍事中心主義から非暴力紛争解決への過渡期にあって、UNSGは日本や日本の例にならおうとする他の国々に対し、代替奉仕サービスを提供することで安んじて世界平和や公正に貢献しうるという保証を与えることができる。

勝守寛博士は最近、すべての国が毎年ある一定の割合で軍事費をへらし、その節約分を国連の平和維持、戦争防止、非暴力的な紛争解決活動に当てる、という方式を提案している。[15]同博士はまた、国連の平和維持活動も、私のUNSG構想と同じく、国連職員の指揮のもとに、あらゆる国からのボランティアから成り立つものにすべきだと提案、日本の若者が憲法9条を侵すことなく参加できる道を開いている。

良心的参戦拒否国家としての日本

この第9条をめぐる一大討論の中で、日本をもって「良心的参戦拒否国」ないしは英語の頭文字をとって「CO国家」と呼んでいる人々がいる。社民党の現党首、土井たか子代議士、本書の訳者で前参議院議員の國弘正雄教授、作家でベトナム戦争時代の活動家たる小田実氏、広島修道大学の岡本三夫教授らの人々が何れもこれらの着想を用いてきた。[16, 17, 18, 19]より最近には、朝日新聞が日本を「良心的参戦拒否国家」と名づけた。[20]私も1993年の訪日時の講演で日本を目指して「良心的参戦拒否国家」と呼ぶことを始めた。[21]

should enable Japanese youth to participate in such UN peace-keeping activities without violating Article 9.

In the transition period from militarist to non-violent conflict resolution methods, the UNSG could assure Japan, and other nations which might choose to join Japan, that they can safely demonstrate their alternative service activities for world peace and justice.

Dr. Hiroshi Katsumori has recently proposed a scheme whereby all nations might systematically reduce their armaments by a specific percentage each year, transferring the savings from smaller national military budgets to the UN for use in peace-keeping, war prevention, and non-violent conflict resolution activities.[15] He also proposes that this UN peace-keeping force, like my UNSG proposal, be made up of volunteers from all nations, under the leadership of UN officers, thus enabling Japanese youth to serve in it without violating Article 9.

Japan As a Conscientious Objector Nation

Some people in this great debate have called Japan a nation of conscientious objectors or a Conscientious Objector (CO) nation. Ms. Takako Doi, Social Democratic Party (SDP) leader; Masao Kunihiro, former member of the Diet; Japanese author and Vietnam war protester Makoto Oda, Hiroshima Shudo University professor Mitsuo Okamoto and others have used these ideas.[16, 17, 18, 19] More recently, the Japanese newspaper, the *Asahi Shimbun*, has spoken of Japan as a "Conscientious Objector Nation."[20] In my paper for our 1993 visit to Japan I also began to refer to Japan as a Conscientious Objector nation.[21]

良心的参戦拒否への感慨

　多くの西欧社会にあっては、軍務に召集され戦争で殺しもしくは殺されることを求められた際に、殺りくからの免除措置を主張しうる。これら戦争協力を拒む個人は、良心的参戦拒否者と呼ばれ、ふつう軍務に代わるに代替奉仕サービスの提供をもって軍務を免除される。過去においてはこのCOの資格は、多くの場合、汝殺すなかれという宗教上の事由で認められた。ところが最近刊行された『新しい良心的参戦拒否者の像・聖から俗への抵抗の移り変り』という著書の中で、チャールズ・C・モスコスとジョン・W・チェインバーズ2世とは、CO資格の付与が、昔は純粋に宗教上の理由であったものが今日では世俗的なものに移ってきたここ数十年間の経緯を跡づけた。[22] この共著者はまた、このところCOの数が驚くほどの伸びを示していることを明らかにしている。たとえばアメリカ1国に限っても、第1次第2次大戦にあっては、CO免除の率は100人の新兵につき0.15でしかなかったものが、60年代には激増し、ベトナム戦争が長びくにつれ70年代も増加率はひきつづき、1972年には、免除率は100人の新兵につき131に達した。

　現にこの共著は、アメリカがベトナムからの撤収を余儀なくされた理由の1つは、CO免除の激増のために、殺し殺されるための必要な員数を揃えることが難しくなったからだと指摘している。

　良心的参戦拒否というのは、ひとことでいえば、個人が抗議することで、国の戦争遂行行動に影響を与えるための非暴力行為、の謂である。戦争を宣してはみたものの、だれも戦いに顔を出さないというくらい、戦争システムにとって脅威になることはありえない。

　個人次元の参戦拒否が国家の軍事力展開能力にどの程度まで待ったをかけうるかについては、ドイツの事例が興味ぶか

Reflections on Conscientious Objection

Individuals in many Western societies, when faced with being conscripted into military service and required to kill and be killed in war may claim exemption from the slaughter. These non-cooperating individuals are called "conscientious objectors," and are usually allowed to perform alternative service in place of military service. In the past, CO status was granted mostly for religious objection to the killing of one's fellow humans. However, in their recent book, *The New Conscientious Objectors: From Sacred to Secular Resistance*," Charles C. Moskos and John W. Chambers II document a shift, over the past several decades, in the reasons for granting CO status from formerly purely religious ones to secular ones today.[22] They also show an amazing growth in the number of conscientious objectors over the years. To illustrate, for just the United States: in World Wars I and II, the CO exemption rate was about 0.15 exemptions per 100 inductions. This figure rose sharply in the 1960s and on into the 1970s as the Vietnam War grew. By 1972 the exemption rate in America had peaked at 131 exemptions per 100 inductions. Moskos' and Chambers' book suggests that, indeed, one of the reasons why the USA felt compelled to withdraw from Vietnam was this massive rise in CO exemptions which made it difficult to get the necessary men to do the killing and dying.

Conscientious objection in essence is a non-violent action by individuals to protest and have an impact on the course of a nation's war-making acts. What could be more threatening to the war system than to have a war declared and have nobody show up to fight it?

Germany presents an interesting example of the power of individual conscientious objection in limiting a state's ability

い。ドイツは若者を徴兵に引っぱるが、ドイツ基本法は良心的参戦拒否の権利を基本的には認めており、軍部の将軍たちは、国家指導者の軍事的な指示に従うことが困難となる可能性を怖れている。[23] 1996年の徴兵義務制によって徴集された若者の大部分は軍務に就くよりは、代替奉仕サービスを選ぶことがはっきりした。[24]

第2次大戦後のドイツ基本法に盛られた戦争に関する法律上の禁止命令は、日本国憲法の9条ほどには明確ではない。残念なことだが、軍事中心路線に立ち戻りたいという希求にかられ、アメリカの後押しをも得て、ドイツの憲法裁判所は最近戦争や暴力に対する憲法上の制約に手心を加えてしまった。1994年同裁判所は、ドイツがその軍隊をNATOもしくは国連の平和維持活動のためにもし必要なら戦闘行為を含めて、またしてもドイツ国外に派遣しうるという憲法解釈を下した。国会の単純大多数の承認が得られる限りは、である。[25]

良心的参戦拒否は個人だけのもの、という意見も

日本人の中には国家向けのCO資格なんて、と馬鹿にするものがいる。現に読売新聞は朝日新聞の1995年5月3日付けの「非軍事こそ共存の道」と題した社説を批判した。「われわれは国家と個人とが違うことを知ってはいるが、われわれは比喩的にいうなら良心的参戦拒否国家たらんと願っている」というのが朝日の社説だった。[26, 27]

読売はさらに言葉を継ぎ、朝日の提案はたしかに比喩的なものではあるが、道徳や宗教や信条などは個人にかかわる概念であり、国家の安全保障と同じ次元で論ずるのは不可能である、と断じていた。

to use military force. Although Germany conscripts its youth, the German constitution grants a basic right to conscientious objection, and German generals fear that they may have difficulty carrying out military commitments made by the country's leaders.[23] The 1996 compulsory draft found that the majority of young Germans called up to serve chose alternative social service rather than military service.[24]

The legal injunctions against war in Germany's post-World War II constitution are not nearly so eloquently expressed as Japan's Article 9. Unfortunately, in their desire to climb back on a militarist path, which was reinforced by the United States, Germany's Constitutional Court recently seriously compromised its constitutional prohibitions against war and violence. In 1994 the Court interpreted its constitution as permitting Germany to send its soldiers around the world, outside its borders once again, on NATO and/or UN peace-keeping operations, including combat if necessary, so long as a simple majority of the Parliament approved.[25]

Conscientious Objection Only For Individuals, Say Some

Some in Japan ridicule the idea of CO status for a nation. The *Daily Yomiuri* attacked the *Asahi Shimbun* for its May 3, 1995, editorial, "A path toward nonmilitary contribution to the world," in which the *Asahi* said that though we are aware that a nation differs from an individual, we aspire to a nation that is, figuratively speaking, a conscientious objector.[26, 27]

The *Yomiuri* continued by saying that although the *Asahi* made the proposal figuratively, morality, religion and creeds are concepts related to the individual. It is impossible to debate the matter on the same order as national security.

モスコスとチェインバーズの共著ですでに見たように、良心的参戦拒否という概念自体が変化しつつある。彼らが説くごとく、良心的参戦拒否の重心は、伝統的に平和志向のつよい周辺的な教会から、より主流派の教会へと移り、さらには増大する一方のグループへと拡がったが、彼らの軍務の拒否は、ヒューマニズムないしは個人的な事由にのみ基づいている。このような変化の過程をさらに押し進めていくと、CO資格が個人から国民へと移っていくのも、この論理的な前進の延長線上にしかない、といえる。

　憲法9条が生まれるまでというもの、どの国も良心的参戦拒否国家たる理論的根拠を有してはいなかった。良心的参戦拒否という慣行を個人次元から国家次元に拡げていくとは、まさに創造性に富んだ、感動的な着想であった。CO資格が若者の間で極端に伸びているという事実は、文化面での規範が世界規模で変化しつつあることを反映して、ユニークな機会を提供している。世界で最初の真のCO国家として、経済的に強力な日本は、全地球にとって希望にあふれる文化面での新しい規範を形づくる機会にも恵まれているのである。

　国家と若者の双方にCOになるよう力づけることで、戦争に終止符を打ち、平和と公正のために、有意義かつ不可欠な非暴力非軍事の代替奉仕サービスを行っていけるなんて、何とすばらしい挑戦であろうか。

　日本やCO国家としてその後を襲おうとする国々は、壮大な国際的な実験の参加者とみなされることになろう。それは紛争解決への非暴力非軍事的なアプローチが探究され開発される実験場であり、やがてはすべての国と国連によって利用されることになる。そうすることでわれわれは新しい一千年期を迎えるにあたり、紛争解決のための暴力的な手段から非暴力なそれへの転換が可能となる。

　この種の機構造りにかけてはアメリカに先例がある。アメ

As we have already seen from Moskos and Chamber, concepts of conscientious objection are changing. As these authors say, the center of gravity of conscientious objection has moved from the traditional peace churches to the more inclusive mainstream religious denominations to an ever-widening group for whom objection to military service is based solely upon humanistic or private motives. Continuing this process of change to include the expansion of CO status from the individual to the nation is simply the next step in this logical progression.

Until Article 9 was born, no nation had any rationale for claiming to be a Conscientious Objector nation. What a creatively inspiring idea it is to expand this practice of conscientious objection from the level of the individual to the level of the nation. The radical growth of CO status among young people reflects worldwide changes in cultural norms and presents a unique opportunity. As the world's first truly Conscientious Objector nation, economically powerful Japan has the opportunity to shape a hopeful new cultural norm for the entire planet. What a magnificent challenge—to put an end to war by encouraging both nation and youth to become COs, and to do meaningful and essential, alternative, non-violent, non-military service for peace and justice.

Japan, and other nations seeking to follow her path as a CO nation, might be looked upon as participants in a kind of grand international experiment in which non-violent, non-military approaches to conflict resolution are explored and developed for ultimate use by all nations and the United Nations, so that we can move into the new millennium and a transition from violent to non-violent means for resolving conflict.

There is a precedent for this kind of institution building

リカを形成する50の州は、しばしば社会・経済・政治面での実験場として機能し、現に連邦政府は州次元の立法・政策面での実験の成果を国家レベルの目的のために借用してきた。[28]だから日本やコスタリカ、それに後刻CO国家に加わるいくつかの国々が「実験的に」他者の手本となるような非暴力問題解決者になることで、他国や国連のために緊急なサービスを提供している姿を予測することもできようというものだ。

　暴力から非暴力への移行はきわめてひよわであるばかりか、ヒトという種の生き残りのために重要きわまりないので、きちんと根付くよう大切に保護育成されねばならない。

CO資格への移行を助ける

　十全なCO国家という資格に移行する上で、日本には地球の人々、世界の他国の指導者たち、それに国連の力づけや助力を受ける資格もあればそれを必要としてもいる。ひとたび日本がこの新しい文化面での規範に道をつけたなら、この路線に加わることを欲する他の国々へも勇気づけと助力とが与えられてしかるべきである。いろいろな恩典が付与されることで、あえてこの新しい路線をとることを願っている日本や他の国々を動機づけることが可能となろう。

　この新路線への必要が国事として肝要であるばかりか、国際関係における戦争と暴力の支配にすっかり馴らされてしまったお互いの胸中で、安全保障への関心がどれほど大きい地位を占めているかを思うと、CO国家たらんと願っている国々に対しては、安全保障面での何らかの保障が与えられてしかるべきである。たとえば日本が自衛隊の規模を着実に削減縮小していくと同時に代替奉仕サービスの種類を充実していくにともない、諸外国が安全保障面での日本人の懸念を和

in America. The fifty states of the United States have often acted as socio-economic-political experimental laboratories from which the federal government has been able to borrow and adapt from state legislative and policy experiments for use nationally.[28] Thus I can imagine Japan, Costa Rica, and later a few other Conscientious Objector nations performing an urgent service for the rest of the nations and the UN by being world-class "experimental" non-violent conflict resolvers from which we all might learn.

Because this transition from violence to non-violence is so fragile and important for our species' survival, it must be protected and nurtured so that its roots grow strong.

Assisting the Transition to CO Status

To successfully change to full-fledged CO nation status, Japan deserves and needs the encouragement and assistance of Earth's people, leaders of the world's other nations, and the United Nations. Once Japan has pioneered this new cultural norm, other nations wishing to join this path should be encouraged and assisted in so doing. Offering several kinds of incentives could motivate Japan and other nations wishing to take this significant new route.

Because there is such an urgent need for this new path in the affairs of nations, and since security concerns loom large in the minds of most of us who have been conditioned by the rule of war and violence in international affairs, some kind of security assurance arrangements should be made available to those nations seeking to be CO nations. For example, as Japan steadily reduces the size of its SDF and simultaneously increases its alternative service offerings, the

らげるべく、UNSGグループの支援による援護を暫定措置として提供するなどの方策がとられてよい。なおこのUNSGについては本章の前段ですでに取り上げておいた。

　なおCO国家を支援するためのいくつかの奨励策の中には、特別な通商上の恩恵措置、資源確保能力の強化、市民の移動に関する特権その他が考えられよう。

CO国家にとっての代替奉仕サービス

　紛争処理にとって、それが国際的であると否とにかかわりなく、戦争と暴力とが不適切な手段でしかないことは、とくに殺戮と破壊のための科学技術面での能力がこれほどまでに巨大化した時代にあっては、自明のことである。民族・部族・宗教レベルでの紛争が軍事力をもってしては解決しかねることを、いまやわれわれは身につけるに至った。何か新しい方途を真剣に探し求めねばならない。

　非暴力的な紛争解決や戦争防止活動の訓練を受け技能を有する専門家によって可能とされる開かれた対話こそが、紛争処理、戦争防止、ならびに平和と公正のための新しいモデルになっていかなければならない。「紛争の平和的処理」と題された国連憲章の第4章は、紛争解決のための非暴力的な接近方法のいくつかを掲げているが、交渉、調査、仲介、和解、斡旋、それに司法的解決がこれである。

　紛争を解決もせず、社会・文化・自然に相わたる環境を汚染し、人間、天然、経済面での貴重な資源を大量に浪費するばかりが能の暴力的な軍事措置に、世界は年間1兆ドルにも上る巨費を費消している。[29] それに反し、非暴力的な手だて自身や、紛争解決のための非暴力的な手段についてお互いを啓蒙していく上には、1文も使っていないのに等しい。いまや世界は、少数でもよい真底から献身的なCO国家が、生き残りのための道筋を他者への手本として示すべく、非暴力的な

rest of the world ought to allay Japanese security fears by providing transition protection with United Nations Security Group support, discussed earlier in this chapter.

A few additional incentives to encourage CO nations might include special trade privileges, resource availability enhancements, and citizen mobility privileges.

Alternative Service For Conscientious Objector Nations

War and violence are inappropriate for trying to settle disputes, international or otherwise, especially in the modern era of massive scientific and engineering designs for killing and destruction. We learn anew from the world's contemporary ethnic-tribal-religious conflicts that military force cannot resolve these disputes. We must seriously try something new. Open dialogue facilitated by persons trained and skilled in nonviolent conflict resolution and war prevention activities must become our new models for settling disputes, preventing war, and restoring peace and justice. Chapter VI of the United Nation's Charter, "Pacific Settlements of Disputes," suggests several non-violent approaches for resolution of conflict, such as negotiation, enquiry, mediation, conciliation, arbitration, and judicial settlement.

The world currently spends about a trillion dollars per year on violent military measures that do not resolve conflict, that pollute the social, cultural, and natural environment, and that waste vast quantities of precious resources—human, natural, and financial.[29] Yet, the world spends practically nothing on non-violent measures, or in educating us in non-violent means of conflict resolution. The world needs a few seriously dedicated Conscientious Objector nations to demonstrate

国民レベルでの代替奉仕サービスを設けることを必要としている。

　この「国民レベルでの代替奉仕サービス」とは、それぞれの国が、(1) 戦争と暴力との根本的な原因を減少させ、(2) お互いがかかえる不可避な紛争を非暴力の形で解決していく方途を教えてくれるような、多種多様な活動を指している。

代替奉仕サービスについての具体的提案

　代替奉仕サービスについてそれを口にするだけでは不十分である。具体性をもった個別的で有用しかも現実的な方策が講じられなければ、諸国家がいま手にしている戦争暴力サイドの巨大な選択肢の累積にとてもたちうちできない。戦争や軍事的暴力への、具体的で血の通った代替案がわれわれの側に枯渇しているという事態は、今日のハイテク社会の実体を反映する悲しい事実である。憲法9条が日本のものである以上、日本人こそ他からの助勢も仰いだ上で、自国政府に対し、国民レベルでの代替奉仕サービスの具体案を提示するという大きな責務を負っている、というべきであろう。

代替奉仕サービスへの貢献の促進

　われわれの住んでいる世界は、宣伝、促進、広告それに広報の世界である。しばしば諸国家によって戦争と暴力の宣伝に用いられる広報活動だが、[30] 紛争解決における軍事中心主義への代替案についてプラスイメージと展望とを創り出すために使われることだって可能である。日本人の側にそういう意志と動機が存在すれば、の話だが。

　CO路線を進めていくにあたり、日本人は自国政府に対し憲法9条の戦争放棄の実体と、世界平和と公正を目指す日本

non-violent forms of national alternative service as a survival path for all to follow.

By "national alternative service" I mean a vast array of activities by which nations might contribute to (1) a lessening of the root causes of war and violence, and (2) helping all of us learn how to resolve our inevitable conflicts non-violently.

Concrete Alternative Service Proposals

It is not enough for us just to speak about alternative services. Concrete, specific, useful, and practical plans for national alternative service must be developed to match the vast libraries of war-and-violence options that nations presently embrace. It is a sad commentary on today's high technology societies that we are so bankrupt of fleshed-out practical alternatives to war and military violence. Since Article 9 is Japan's, Japanese people, perhaps with help from others, are faced with the major challenge of proposing to their government a multitude of practical and implementable kinds of national alternative service.

Promoting Alternative Service Contributions

We live in a world of propaganda, promotion, advertising, and public relations. While public relations is frequently used by nations to propagandize for war and violence,[30] it can also be used to create positive images and visions of alternatives to the militarist view of conflict resolution—if the will and motivation exist for so doing.

Japanese people must insist that their government, as it moves on a CO path, use public relations massively in this

の非暴力非軍事の代替奉仕サービスについて、大々的な広報活動を行うよう求めていくべきである。憲法9条にまつわるこの種の広報は、堂々と胸を張って、しかも国内向けだけではなく、全世界の人々に対し、悪びれることなく行われるべきである。

朝日新聞によるCO路線への提言

　朝日新聞の1995年5月3日付けが数ページを費やして、日本に憲法と9条の順守を求め、世界平和への非軍事的貢献という路線を、CO国家の一員として追い求めていくことを唱えたと知るのは心づよいかぎりである。[31]

　このテーマについて同紙がその後も何人かの論者に討議させたことは、この重要事項に関する現行の討議を深める上に大きく寄与した。朝日新聞の提言のいくつかは、CO国家による代替奉仕サービスという着想にかかわりをもっている。これらの着想は私の訪日時のいくつかの講演で取り上げたほか、本章の前段でも論じ、次章ではもっと詳細にわたって突っこんでいる。朝日の提言中に盛られた6つの分野は概ね以下のようなもので、これらの提言の詳細な検討については、本書の補遺 (1) を参照されたい。

1. 国際協力法を制定し対外援助をかさあげする。

2. 平和支援隊を創成、在来型の平和維持活動に従事させる。

3. 理想主義的な憲法9条は改定の必要はない。

4. 自衛隊を段階的に削減、自国防衛のためだけのものに改造する。

positive way to tell the story of Article 9's renunciation of war, and of the nation's non-violent, non-military alternative services for world peace and justice. This story must be proudly told not only to Japanese people, but also, without apology, to all people around the world.

The Asahi Shimbun's Proposed Conscientious Objector Path

It was encouraging to learn from the several pages of ideas presented by the *Asahi Shimbun* in its May 3, 1995, edition that they too are calling for Japan to honor its Constitution and Article 9, as a Conscientious Objector nation by pursuing a path of non-military contributions for world peace.[31] Discussion of these ideas by others in subsequent editions of this newspaper also made important contributions to the ongoing debate on these important matters. Several of the *Asahi Shimbun* proposals relate to ideas of alternative service for CO nations—ideas that I have discussed in past visits to Japan and which are presented in this chapter and explored in more detail in the next. Below are the six broad general sectors in their proposal. (Elaboration of these proposals can be found in Appendix 1.)

1. Enact an International Cooperation Law to upgrade external assistance.

2. Create a Peace Support Corps for taking part in traditional peace-keeping operations.

3. Idealistic Article 9 of the Constitution does not need to be revised.

4. Scale down the Self-Defense Forces into a force exclusively for defending the country.

5. 冷戦型の安保を、アジア全地域の平和に力点をおく。

6. 国際連合を改革し、より健全な国際機関への改組の先頭に立つ。

朝日新聞の提言への論評

　本書で論ずる詳細の多くは朝日提言が表明した考え方と合致する。私はその提言と所論のほとんどに賛成である。ただ多少ちがうのは、朝日が憲法9条は自衛権を否定するものではない、としている点である。自衛権は国家の基本的な権利である、というのが彼らの主張である。かりにその通りだとして、自衛権とは軍事力に基づくものと限定すべきであろうか、という疑問は残る。

　朝日提言が、冷戦終結にともなう脅威の減少に見合った自衛隊の削減を求めている点はみごとだが、軍事力を唯一の「力」とみなしている点は正しくない。自衛のためにあるいは使用可能な「力」は軍事力以外の形でも厳存する。その一例はマハトマ・ガンジーのいう「サチャグラハ」すなわち「真理の力」[32] である。マーチン・ルーサー・キング師は「魂の力」[33] と呼んでいる。いま1つは「市民ベースの防衛」で、これについては次章で触れる。

　自衛隊が着実にその規模を縮小していくにともない、日本が「市民ベースの防衛」のために人員の訓練や装備の充実を同時進行させては、と私は言いたい。

　日本国憲法がはたして軍事力による防衛を認めているかどうかについては、異論が存在する。よしんば憲法の文言が軍事力による自衛の権利を認めていることが疑いもない確かさで証明されたとしても、憲法9条は法律で戦争放棄を決めた、しかも普遍性をもったすばらしい先例であり、日本が追求し

5. Overcome security arrangements for the Cold War and give emphasis to peace in Asia as a whole.

6. Take the initiative for reforming the United Nations into a healthier world body.

Commentary on the Asahi Shimbun Proposals

Many details in this book fit well with the ideas the *Asahi Shimbun* has put forth. I agree with most of their proposals and arguments. I differ with them somewhat in their argument that Article 9 does not deny the right of self-defense, which they say is the basic right of a state. Assuming that this is correct, must we necessarily conclude that self-defense has to be based on military force? The *Asahi* proposal admirably seeks to substantially reduce the SDF in size commensurate with the threats that exist in the post-Cold War era, but incorrectly assumes that military force is the only kind of force available. There are other forms of force which might be used by a nation to defend itself. One such force is Gandhi's *Satyagraha* or "truth-force."[32] Martin Luther King, Jr. speaks of "soul force."[33] Another is Gene Sharp's Civilian Based Defense, which is touched upon in the next chapter. I would argue that as the SDF is steadily downsized, Japan might wish to simultaneously train and equip its people for Civilian Based Defense.

Of course there is a difference of opinion as to whether or not Japan's constitution permits a military self-defense force. Even if it could be unequivocally demonstrated that the words of the constitution give Japan the right to a military self-defense force, I would still argue that Article 9 is such a universally significant precedent as a legal renunciation

ようとしている非軍事的な防衛の手だては、お互いすべてにとっての将来にわたる手本としてこれを弱体化してはならない、とあえて主張しつづけるものである。

　自衛を看板にする軍隊にとっての厄介きわまりない問題の1つは、自衛がしばしば攻撃になってしまうという現実である。文民であると軍人であるとを問わず、どの社会においてであれ、軍事中心主義者というのは、自衛と攻撃とのちがいを簡単にボカしてしまうというかたむきがある。アメリカもその例に洩れないので、第2次大戦中は、陸軍省<ruby>陸軍省<rt>デパートメント・オブ・ウォー</rt></ruby>としかるべき名を与えられていた政府機関が、いまでは国防省<ruby>国防省<rt>デパートメント・オブ・ディフェンス</rt></ruby>と婉曲語で呼ばれているのなどは、その好例である。近年におけるアメリカによる対外軍事冒険の数々を思うと、国防省というのは実体にそぐわない、誤った呼び名にすぎず、攻撃省<ruby>攻撃省<rt>デパートメント・オブ・オフェンス</rt></ruby>という方がはるかにふさわしいことがはっきりする。1989年のパナマ侵攻にはじまり、グレナダ侵攻、ニカラグアでの内戦幇助、ベトナム戦争、湾岸戦争、とその実例には事欠かない。

　1つはっきりしている有意義な現実とは、いまや日本という主要な経済大国がこの英知をその憲法内に収めとっている、という事実である。これは全人類史を通じての初めてのできごとである。それがどこに由来するかは問題ではない。大事なのは地球市民としてのわれわれが、憲法9条を育み強化し持続する上で日本の兄弟姉妹を支持し勇気づけるべく行動することである。そうすれば、すべての民族国家や国連にとっての「生き残りのための指針」として、来たるべき新しい一千年期において憲法9条が生きて躍動することが可能となろう。

of war, that non-military forms of defense be sought by Japan so as not to weaken it as a model for all our futures.

One of the really serious problems with armed force for so-called self-defense lies in the reality that, frequently, self-defense becomes self-offense. Militarists, civilian or military, in all societies find it terribly easy to blur this line between self-defense and offense. We have seen this problem in the US where we have created a euphemistic name—the Department of Defense (DOD)—for what during World War II was perhaps more appropriately called the Department of War. As we look at many of America's recent foreign adventures such as the 1989 Panama invasion, the Grenada invasion, the Nicaraguan subversion, the Vietnam War, and the Gulf War, some of us think that the DOD has been misnamed—it should be called the Department of Offense.

The significant reality is simply this—for the first time in all of history we have a major economic power, Japan, with this wisdom in its constitution. It makes no difference where it came from. What matters is that we as Earth Citizens act to support and encourage our Japanese sisters and brothers in nurturing, strengthening, and sustaining Article 9 so that it can truly come alive as a survival guide for all nation-states and the United Nations in the new millennium.

註釈

1. 現在日本で行われている憲法9条の将来や国連事項についての論議は健全である。民主主義国にあっては、人々が真理に到達するための過程で、自分たちにとって重要な考え方について探究や討論、選び出しやふりわけの機会をもつことが求められる。いまこの稿をしたためている私は、真理の探究についての美しい文言を思いおこす。マジソンなるウィスコンシン大学の大学院で勉強していたころ、私は大学の歴史的な古い建造物たるバスコムホールにある、青銅製の記念額に刻されていた、以下のことばを思いおこす。因にこの額は「選び出しふりわけ額」と呼ばれ、その文言は1894年の理事者会に由来していた。当時、彼ら理事者は当時の社会にとって重要な問題を俎上（そじょう）にのせることを控えるよう、有力者や強力な団体からの圧力を受けていたのである。この文言は次のようにいたっていた。

   「他所にあっては自由な攻究（こうきゅう）に待ったをかけられるという限界があろうとも、ここ偉大なる州立ウィスコンシン大学にあっては、かの持続的にして恐れを知らない『選び出しやふりわけ』の作業を力づけつづけていかねばならない。そうすることによってのみ真理は発見しうるからである」

   この「選び出しふりわけ」ということばを日本式に焼きなおし、平和憲法前文からの引用を加えて、以下のような文言にすることを提案したい。

   「他所にあっては自由な攻究に待ったをかけられるという限界があろうとも、われわれ主権者としての日本国民は、かの持続的にして恐れを知らない『選び出しやふりわけ』の作業を力づけつづけていかねばならない。そうすることによってのみ真理は発見しうるからである」

2. クラウス・シュリクトマン『平和の倫理学・幣原喜重郎と憲法第9条』ジャパン・フォーラム、国際日本研究ジャーナル　第7巻第1号43〜68ページ。オックスフォード大学出版局刊。同人『21世紀の政治指導者幣原喜重郎（1872年〜1951年）の生涯と外交』日本アジア学会議事録1996年9月。

3. ダグラス・マッカーサー『兵士は語る：陸軍大将ダグラス・マッカーサーの公的文書ならびに演説集』319ページ　1965年　ニューヨーク、フレデリック・プラガー出版社刊。カリフォルニア州ロサンゼルスでのアメリカ在郷軍人協会での、1955年1月26日の講演から。

4. 1951年5月、マッカーサーはトルーマン大統領による解職についてのアメリカ議会公聴会に出席、次のように述べた。

   「そういうわけで核戦争が何を意味するかについて日本人くらいよく知っている国民は他にはいない。彼らにとってはそれは空理空論ではなかったのである。彼らは死者の数を数え、葬送したのだった。彼らは自発的にその憲法に戦争を非合法化する条項を入れたのである。幣原首相が私のところにやって来て次のように口にした。『私は長いことこの問題に対処する唯一の方法は戦争をなくすことだと、考え、信じてきました。』同首相はさらにことばを継ぎ、『軍人としての貴下にこのような話題を持ち出すのは気がひけます。とても受け入れてはくれない、と確信しているからです。でも何とかがんばっていま起草中の憲法に、そのよ

NOTES

1. The present dialogue in Japan as to the future of Article 9 and other related matters is a healthy one. In a democracy, people must have an opportunity to explore and discuss, to sift and winnow ideas of importance to them, as a way of finding truth. As I write this I am reminded of a beautiful set of words on truth seeking that I discovered as a graduate student at the University of Wisconsin, Madison. On the wall of Bascom Hall, one of the historic old campus buildings, there is a large bronze plaque called "The Sifting and Winnowing" plaque. The words on this plaque came from the university's 1894 Board of Regents, when they resisted great pressure from powerful people and institutions to silence discussion of important matters to our society at that time. This plaque reads as follows: "Whatever may be the limitations which trammel inquiry elsewhere, we believe that the great State University of Wisconsin should ever encourage that continual and fearless sifting and winnowing by which alone the truth can be found."

   Let me suggest a modified Japanese "Sifting and Winnowing" plaque with words taken from the Preamble of Japan's Peace Constitution as follows: "Whatever may be the limitations which trammel inquiry elsewhere, we believe that the Sovereign People of Japan should ever encourage that continual and fearless sifting and winnowing by which alone the truth can be found."

2. Schlichtmann, Klaus, "The Ethics of Peace: Shidehara Kijūrō and Article 9 of the Constitution," *Japan Forum, The International Journal of Japanese Studies.* Oxford University Press, Vol. 7, No. 1, Spring 1995, pp. 43–68, and Schlictmann, Klaus, "A Statesman for The Twenty-First Century: The life and Diplomacy of Shidehara Kijūrō (1872–1951)," *Transactions of the Asiatic Society of Japan,* September, 1996.

3. MacArthur, Douglas, *A Soldier Speaks: Public Papers and Speeches of General of the Army, Douglas MacArthur.* New York: Frederick A. Praeger, 1965, p. 319. From a speech to an American veteran's group, the American Legion, on January 26, 1955, in Los Angeles California.

4. In May, 1951, MacArthur addressed the US Congress in Hearings on his firing by President Harry S. Truman. He said, "So the Japanese people, more than any other people in the world, understand what atomic warfare means. It wasn't academic with them. They counted their dead, and they buried them. They, of their own volition, wrote into their constitution a provision outlawing war. When their Prime Minister came to me, Mr. Shidehara, and said: 'I have long contemplated and believed that the only solution with this problem is to do away with war.' He said: 'With great reluctance I advance the subject to you, as a military man, because I am convinced that you would not accept it; but,' he said, 'I would like to endeavor, in the constitution we are drawing up, to put in such a provision.' And I couldn't help getting up

うな条項を入れたいと願っているのです。』と。

　そこで私は思わず立ち上がって、握手を求め彼に対し『それは恐らくはもっともすばらしく建設的な第1歩だと思う』旨を伝え、彼を勇気づけ、かくして第9条が憲法に書き入れられたのです。」

　マッカーサーによる5月5日の軍事委員会外交問題委員会における「極東における軍事情勢」証言。アメリカ上院第82国会第1部会223ページ。1951年5月3、4、5、7、8、9、10、11、14日　政府刊行物センター（ワシントンD.C.）刊。

5. クラウス・シュリクトマン：上掲書

6. 新約聖書マタイ伝：26～52

7. 1993年、B・ガリ国連事務総長（当時）が、軍事作戦を含め自衛隊員を国連の平和維持活動に自由に参加できるよう憲法9条の変更を迫ったのに対し、宮沢喜一首相（当時）が断固として首を縦にふらなかったのは正しかった。
   T.R.リード「B・ガリ総長、日本で兵員募集を」ワシントンポスト紙1993年2月号A28面。

8. 小沢一郎『日本改造計画』94ページ（英語版）
   1994年　東京、講談社インターナショナル刊。

9. 読売新聞「読売憲法私案」1994年11月3日付け1ページ

10 クリストファー・D・ストーン「戦争と環境に関する文化的規範を変える力としての法」アーサー・H・ウェスティング（編）。
   ストックホルム国際平和研究所『文化的規範：戦争と環境』所収
   1988年　オクスフォード、オクスフォード大学出版局刊。

11. 1992年1月東京で開かれた「アジア太平洋における平和軍縮共生シンポ」における、津田塾大学ダグラス・ラミス教授の講演から。

12. カメロン・W・バー「奇妙な軍事的カップルがより緊急な関係をもつべく訓練を」クリスチャン・サイエンス・モニター紙1996年11月20日号10～11ページ。

13. リー・バトラー退役米空軍将軍：1996年12月4日のワシントンD.C.の記者クラブでの発言。

14. ダニエル・スナイダー「核兵器廃絶努力における新しい同盟者」クリスチャン・サイエンス・モニター紙　1996年12月5日号、4ページ。

15. 勝守寛「完全軍備撤廃に至る過渡期における国連による軍備管理。50年間で憲法9条の理想に到達するための軍縮モデル」世界連邦建設同盟名古屋支部と全米世界連邦協会ボストン支部との姉妹関係提携に際してのペーパー。1996年11月3日、全米世界連邦協会ボストン支部において。

and shaking hands with the old man, and telling him that I thought that was one of the greatest constructive steps that could possibly be taken. ... I encouraged him and they wrote that provision in." MacArthur, May 5th Testimony on the Military Situation in the Far East: Hearing before the Committee on Armed Services and the Committee on Foreign Relation, United State Senate, Eighty-Second Congress, First Session, Part 1, May 3, 4, 5, 7, 8, 9, 10, 11, 12 and 14, 1951, US Government Printing Office, Washington, DC, p. 223.

5. Schlichtmann, Klaus, op. cit.

6. Matthew 26:52.

7. Prime Minister Kiichi Miyazawa was right in 1993 to strongly reject UN Secretary General Boutros Boutros-Ghali's urging that Japan change its Article 9 so as to permit the sending of Japanese soldiers freely on UN peace-keeping operations, including military operations. Reid, T. R., "Boutros-Ghali Recruits Soldiers in Japan." *The Washington Post*, 19 February 1993, p. A28.

8. Ozawa, Ichiro, *Blueprint For A New Japan*. Tokyo: Kodansha International, 1994, page 94.

9. *Yomiuri Shimbun*, "*Yomiuri* works out draft of Constitution revision," 3 November 1994, p. 1.

10. Stone, Christopher D., "Chapter 6. The law as a force in shaping cultural norms relating to war and the environment," in Westing, Arthur H. (ed.), *Cultural Norms, War and the Environment*, Stockholm International Peace Research Institute. Oxford: Oxford University Press, 1988.

11. From a talk by Douglas Lummis, Tsuda College, at the January 31–February 1, 1992 "Symposium on Peace, Disarmament, and Symbiosis in the Asia-Pacific Region," Tokyo.

12. Barr, Cameron W., "Military Odd Couple Trains in Tandem To Forge Closer Ties." *The Christian Science Monitor*, 20 November 1996, pp. 10–11.

13. Butler, Lee, General USAF (Ret.), "National Press Club Remarks," 4 December 1996, Washington, DC.

14. Sneider, Daniel, "New Allies in the Bid To Ban Nuclear Arms." *The Christian Science Monitor*, 5 December 1996, p. 4.

15. Katsumori, Hiroshi, "Arms Control by the UN during the Transition to Complete Global Disarmament: A Disarmament Model Attainable to Article Nine's Ideal in 50 Years," a paper for the sister relationship between the Nagoya Chapter of the United World Federalists of Japan and the Boston Chapter of the World Federalist Association, 3 November 1996.

16. メラニー・スレルケルト「日本の平和主義は拱手を許さないと土井たか子氏は語る」とモンタナ州ミズーラ、「モンタナ・カイミン」紙1991年5月22日、3ページ。

17. 國弘正雄「良心的兵役拒否者 (1)、(2)」　クニヒロのアメリカーナ欄スチューデント・タイムス紙　1983年4月22日号、4月29日号。

18. 小田実「ジャパン・アジア・クォータリー・レビュー」34～37ページ1991年。

19. 岡本三夫「核兵器の非合法化に向かって」研究紀要第8巻。1992年　広島修道大学刊。

20. 朝日イブニング社説　1995年5月3日号「世界への非軍事的貢献の途」。

21. チャールズ・オーバービー「世界平和への日本の贈物と非暴力的紛争解決」1993年11月10日から12月12日に至る日本の憲法第9条市民の会ほか平和団体の会合における講演。

22. チャールズ・C・モスコス、ジョン・W・チェイムバーズ（共編）『新しい良心的参戦拒否者・聖なる抵抗から世俗の抵抗へ』オクスフォード大学出版局（ポケット版）。

23. ドイツ連邦共和国基本法（ドイツ憲法）「第1章基本的権利、第4条3、本人の良心に反して何人といえども武器の使用を含む戦争義務に従事させることはない」議会評議会によって公布され1990年8月31日の東西ドイツ統合条約および1990年9月23日の連邦法によって修正される。

24.「ドイツの矛盾」ビジネスウィーク誌　1996年1月15日版　47ページ。

25.「ドイツ憲法裁判所の行動に関する記事」ニューヨークタイムズ紙、1994年6月12日号A1ページ。クリスチャン・サイエンス・モニター紙1994年7月13日号　1ページ。

26. デイリー読売「良心的参戦拒否国家」、1995年6月14日号6ページ。

27. 朝日イブニング・上掲紙。

28. 1例をあげると、ウィスコンシン州は20世紀の初頭に先進的ないくつかの社会立法を先駆的に成立させたが、のちに至り、1930年代の内憂の時期に連邦政府によって形を変え採用された。失業保険などの社会的立法が脳裏に浮かぶ。

29. ルース・L・シバード:『世界の軍事・社会支出1991年度』ワールド・プライオリティーズ（ワシントンD.C.）1991年11ページ。

30. 広報活動が戦争や平和に関する一般国民の考え方に強力に影響しうることは、1991年ペルシア湾岸石油資源戦争の直前に、宣伝としての広報活動が収めた成果から容易に見てとることができる。アメリカ国民を悲憤慷慨させ、50万人の将兵を中東に派遣し「われわれの」石油資源の供給

16. Threlkeld, Melanie, "Doi says Japan's pacifism no excuse to relax," *Montana Kaimin*, Missoula, Montana, May 22, 1991, p. 3.

17. Kunihiro, Masao: Consientions Objector (1) & (2): Kunihiro's Americana 586 & 587. The Student Times, Tokyo Japan, April 22 & April 29, 1983, p. 16 & 17.

18. Oda, Makoto, "A Nation of Conscientious Objectors," *AMPO, Japan-Asia Quarterly Rev.*, Vol. 23, No. 1, 1991, pp. 34–37.

19. Okamoto, Mitsuo, "Towards the Delegitimization of Nuclear Weapons," *Research Review*, Hiroshima Shudo University, Vol. 8, 1992.

20. *Asahi Evening News* editorial, "A path toward nonmilitary contribution to the world," 3 May, 1995.

21. Overby, Charles, "Article 9: Japan's Gift For World Peace And Nonviolent Conflict Resolution," paper presented to Japanese Article 9 Society Citizen and Peace group meetings in Japan, Nov. 10–Dec. 12, 1993.

22. Moskos, Charles C., and Chambers II, John W., (eds.), *The New Conscientious Objectors: From Sacred to Secular Resistance*. Oxford University Press, 1993 (paperback).

23. The German Constitution, Basic Law for the Federal Republic of Germany, "I. BASIC RIGHTS, Article 4 (3) No one may be compelled against his conscience to render war service involving the use of arms." Promulgated by the Parliamentary Council and Amended by the Unification Treaty of 31 August 1990 and Federal Statute of 23 September 1990, p. 9.

24. "German Ambivalence," *Business Week*, 15 January 1996, p. 47.

25. Reports on the German Constitutional Court's actions on July 12, 1994, *The New York Times*, p. A1, 13 July 1994 and *The Christian Science Monitor*, p. 1, 13 July 1994.

26. *Daily Yomiuri*, "A Conscientious Objector Nation?," 14 June 1995, No. 6.

27. *Asahi*, op. cit.

28. For example, the state of Wisconsin pioneered in several forms of progressive social legislation early in the 20th Century which were later adapted and adopted by the federal government during the trauma of the 1930s. Unemployment compensation and other forms of social legislation come to mind.

29. Sivard, Ruth L., *World Military And Social Expenditures 1991*. World Priorities, Box 25140, Washington, DC 20007, 1991, p. 11.

30. The power of public relations to influence people's attitudes on matters of war and peace can easily be seen from a recent application of it as propaganda, just prior to the 1991 Persian Gulf oil-resource war. In order to get the American people aroused, angry, and motivated to support the sending of

を守ることへの支持をとりつけるべく、クウェート政府は1990年の秋に大手のPR会社と契約、アメリカ国民と議会向けに、イラクの暴力と獣性とを売りこませた。

テレビの画面や新聞雑誌の紙面に、かわいらしくいかにも正直そうな15歳のクウェートの少女がしばしば顔を見せ、イラク兵士が病院の保温器から赤ん坊を取り出し、床に叩きつけて死に至らしめた次第を語るのだった。このシーンはブッシュ大統領によるイラク軍の残虐行為とやらの申し立てとピタリだった。何人かの連邦上院議員、それにアムネスティーの関係者ですらがこのホラ話を信じこんだ。この宣伝費用をだれが負担したのかは、公開されなかったし、この15歳の少女が実は駐米クウェート大使サウド・ナシア・アルサバの娘、ナイラーであることも発表されなかった。後に調べたところでは少女の話は恐らくホラであった。でも戦端が開かれるまでに、アメリカ人はすっかり反イラク宣伝にイカれて、サダム・フセインなる悪玉をこらしめる唯一の手だては戦争だとして、開戦を圧倒的大多数が支持するに至っていた。

ヒトラーの宣伝相たるゲッベルスは、第2次大戦前夜また大戦中の日本の宣伝担当者と同じく、この手の広報宣伝活動のもつ影響力の大きさを承知していた。

ジョン・R・マッカーサーの「クウェートの証人ナイラーを忘れるな」ニューヨーク・タイムス紙対論欄　1992年1月6日、A17ページ。

同じく『第2戦線・湾岸戦争における検閲と宣伝』1992年　バークレー、カリフォルニア大学出版部。

ジョアン・リップマン「ヒル・＆・ノールトン社はその広報戦術の故に新たに攻撃さる」ウォール・ストリート・ジャーナル誌1992年1月7日版B6ページ。

31. 朝日　掲載紙。

32. モハンダス・K・ガンジー「サチャグラハ教理の起源」　マルフォード・Q・シブレー（編）『静かなる戦い・非暴力抵抗の理論と実践に関する書きもの』　シカゴ、クアドアングル叢書、1963年　ダブルディ・アンカー社。

33. デドーレ・マレイン（編）
『私の夢見る子どもたちを生かすためのことば・アフリカ系アメリカ人の引用句事典』280ページ。1995年　ニューヨーク、ダブルディ社。
マーチン・ルーサー・キング2世はこういっている。
「われわれは自分のもっともきびしい相手に対峙してこういえなければならない。あなたの人に苦しみを与える能力とわれわれの苦しみを受け入れる能力とをすりあわせることにする。あなたの物理的な力を魂の力_{ソウル・フォース}で受けとめるというわけだ」

half a million troops to protect "our" oil supply in the Middle East, the Kuwaiti government hired a large American public relations firm in the fall of 1990 to sell to the US Congress and the American people a story of Iraqi violence and bestiality. On our TV sets and in our newspapers and magazines we saw a lovely and believable fifteen-year-old Kuwaiti girl telling us of Iraqi soldiers taking Kuwaiti babies from their incubators in hospitals and throwing them on the floor to die. This story fit with President Bush's allegations of atrocities by Iraqi forces. Several US senators, and even Amnesty International, believed this tale of terror. We were not told who paid for this propaganda, nor that this fifteen-year-old girl, named Nayirah, was the daughter of Kuwaiti Ambassador to the USA Saud Nasir al-Sabah. Subsequent research indicates that the story was probably untrue. By the time the war actually began, Americans had been propagandized into overwhelmingly supporting the war as the only way to deal with the evil Saddam Hussein. Hitler's Goebbels, as did Japanese propagandists prior to and during World War II, knew of the power of this kind of public relations propaganda.

MacArthur, John R., "Remember Nayirah, Witness for Kuwait" *The New York Times*, OP-ED, 6 January 1992, p. A17; MacArthur, John R., *Second Front: Censorship And Propaganda In The Gulf War*. Berkeley: University of California Press, 1992; and Lipman, Joanne, "Hill & Knowlton Faces New Attacks Over Its PR Tactics," *The Wall Street Journal*, 7 January 1992, p. B6.

31. *Asahi,* op. cit.

32. Gandhi, Mohandas K., "The Origins of Satyagraha Doctrine," in Sibley, Mulford Q. (ed.), *The Quiet Battle: Writings on the Theory and Practice of Non-Violent Resistance*. Chicago: Quadrangle Books, Doubleday Anchor, 1963.

33. Mullane, Deirdre (ed.), *Words To Make My Dream Children Live: A Book Of African American Quotations*. New York: Doubleday, 1995, p. 280. Martin Luther King, Jr. said, "Somehow we must be able to stand up against our most bitter opponents and say, 'We shall match your capacity to inflict suffering by our capacity to endure suffering. We will meet your physical force with soul force.'"

放射能物質の人体実験をされた人々。誰も、「自由と民主主義の国」アメリカを疑うことなんてできなかった。（アメリカ、ワシントン州）

People who were unknowingly used in radiation experiments. No one could believe that America, the land of freedom and democracy, could do such a thing. (Washington State, USA)

「良心的参戦拒否国家」にとっての代替奉仕サービス

ALTERNATIVE SERVICE FOR A CONSCIENTIOUS OBJECTOR NATION

> 非暴力というのは強力かつ公正な武器である。
> これは歴史的にもユニークな武器である。
> それは切っても傷つけることはなく、
> それを振るう人間を高貴にし、
> 剣ではあっても癒す働きをもつ。
>
> マーチン・ルーサー・キング2世[1]

　本章においては、この本の前段で明らかにした代替奉仕サービスに関するいくつかの考え方を素描することにする。これらの可能性についてしゃべったり書いたりするだけでは十分ではない。この種の、またそれ以外の関連する多くの活動を組織化し、日本政府による実施を通じてそれを完成に導いていくという大変な仕事は、未完成のまま残っている。

　日本人にとってもっとも意義のある責務は、数多くの現実的で実行可能な案や行動計画を策定、それを具体的な形で肉づけし、政府をして、新しい非暴力的な形での国際的なリー

Nonviolence is a powerful and just weapon.
It is a weapon unique in history, which cuts without
wounding, and ennobles the man who wields it.
It is a sword that heals.

Martin Luther King, Jr. [1]

This chapter will elaborate in a preliminary way on the several broad ideas for alternative service identified earlier. It is not enough to just talk or write about these possibilities. The hard work of fully developing these and a host of other related activities, and of bringing them to fruition through implementation by the Japanese government, remains to be done.

Japanese people's most significant challenge is to develop and flesh out in very concrete detail a multitude of practical and implementable plans and modes of operation to be fol-

ダーシップを振るうことを得せしむることにある。

　残念ながら、非暴力非軍事的な紛争解決路線は、各国政府が従来歩んできた路線ではない。歴史的にみると、ことを最終的に決めるのは、しょせんは軍事力や暴力でしかない、とするうずきは強力かつわれわれを搦めとりやすい。したがって日本国民がよほどの決意と献身とを示し、憲法に由来する主権者としての権利を断固として行使しないかぎり、自国政府に対し非暴力非軍事的な代替奉仕サービスこそが妥当かつ名誉ある方向性であると選択するよう主張しつづけることはできない。

　1991年の湾岸戦争時には、日本はあの石油資源戦争に兵士を送らず、憲法9条をそのままに守りぬいていこうと努めたあまりに、国際社会からあからさまかつ陰微な形で批難された。ガリ国連事務総長は湾岸戦争のちょうど2年後に、日本は憲法9条を変え、平和維持活動に参加できるようにすべきであると、具体的な提案を行った。[2]

　湾岸戦争が日本にとって事態を厄介にしたのは、日本が中近東の石油資源に大きく依存している点である。しかしながら憲法9条が日本にとってユニークかつ重要な宝物であることを思うと、自国のためにも他国にとってもモデルである第9条を育み維持していくことに悪びれるべきではない。日本の他国への石油依存度が高いならなおのこと、再生可能な、環境を汚さずに済む代替エネルギー、たとえば太陽熱のごときの、開発と商品化に、その創造性に富む最大の資源たる人材をフルに活用し、自国と発展途上世界の益を計るべきであり、それこそはもっとも有意義かつ非暴力的な平和と正義とのCO国家としての寄与たりうる。

　人類の歴史において軍事的暴力こそは長らく決定的な手法であった。したがってこの領域においては多くの材料と原体

lowed by their government in this new, non-violent model of international leadership.

Unfortunately, non-violent and non-military forms of conflict resolution are not paths that governments have commonly trod. Historically, the urge for military force and violence as the ultimate arbiter is powerful and addictive. Therefore, it will take a huge measure of determination and commitment by Japanese people, firmly exercising their constitutional right of sovereignty, to insist that their government choose this new path of non-violent, non-military alternative service as its legitimate and honorable course.

In the 1991 Persian Gulf War, there was both direct and subtle international criticism of Japan for trying to honor the integrity of its Article 9 by not sending soldiers to that resource war. UN Secretary General, Boutros Boutros-Ghali, two years after the Gulf War, specifically suggested that Japan change Article 9 so as to permit it to fully participate in peace-keeping operations.[2]

The Gulf War issue is complicated by Japan's own heavy dependence on Middle-East oil resources. Japan's Article 9, however, is such a unique and important treasure that Japan should never apologize to anyone for seeking to nurture and sustain Article 9 for itself and as a model for all. Japan's dependence on other people's oil should drive it to use its greatest creative resource, its people, to develop and commercialize renewable non-polluting alternative energy paths, such as solar, for itself and for the developing world, as one of its most significant non-violent contributions for peace and justice as a Conscientious Objector nation.

Because military violence has been the dominant mode for much of recorded history, society has a vast reservoir of

験とが蓄積されている。それと比べると、紛争を非暴力的な手だてで対処していくことに関しては、手にできるものは比較的少ない。非暴力を唱える指導者や先駆者は少なくなかったが、非暴力の手段を文字化し機構化し、われわれの社会的文化的文脈に織りこむ点においてはたしかに怠りがあった。軍事中心主義的なやり方と非軍事的なやり方との間には巨大なみぞが横たわっているが、それを埋めていく作業も巨大である。一体どこから手を付けたらよいのだろうか。

各宗教の開祖や実践者は平和への非暴力的な道筋を明らかにしてきた。ただ、権力ゲームは腐敗することにお互い注意することが肝要である。諸宗教や宗教指導者は、軍事中心主義や暴力支配を、受容できる社会的行動としてそのまま支持してきた。たとえば最初の3世紀というもの、初期キリスト教は平和愛好的な宗教であった。が、古代ローマのコンスタンティン1世が十字架の大旆のもとに戦いに勝ちを収めたのがきっかけとなって事態は一変した。紀元前313年、彼はミラノ勅令を発布し、キリスト教をローマの国教と定め、その結果キリスト教は堕落していく。

非暴力理論と実践面での指導者の説くところは、われわれがCO資格を助勢し、日本向けの代替奉仕サービスの具体案を創りあげる上に、参考になる点が多々ある。

われわれはまずポスト冷戦の現代にあって意見の不一致や不調和を生む基本的な要素が何であるかを措定かつ理解し、その上で、これらのマイナス要因を柔らげ取り除くために、CO国家として取り上げるべき前向きで建設的な非暴力行動が何であるかを具体的に措定していかねばならない。たとえば、貧困、人口過剰、豊かな国による過大な消費、宗教上民族上の差異、環境面での大惨禍、資源枯渇、不完全就業、若者の倦怠と疎外、国際的な武器移転、これらはCO国家による数々のありうべき非暴力的行動の可能性を示唆する。

materials and experience in this domain. In comparison, relatively little is available on non-violent means for coping with conflict. While there have been many leaders and pioneers for non-violence over the years, we have been very negligent at codifying and institutionalizing non-violent means into our social and cultural fabric. Much must be done to close this immense gap between militarist modes and non-militarist ones. Where do we start?

Founders and practitioners of religions have articulated non-violent paths for peace. We must be careful, however, for the game of power corrupts. Religions and religious leaders have frequently supported militarism and the rule of violence as acceptable social behavior. Indeed, for the first three centuries, early Christianity was a pacifist religion. This changed when the Roman Emperor Constantine I, after winning a battle under the banner of the cross, issued the Edict of Milan in the year 313 A.D., thus corrupting Christianity by making it the official Roman state religion.

Leaders in non-violence theory and practice offer much from which we might borrow to encourage conscientious objector status and to create alternative service options for Japan.

We must seek to identify and understand the fundamental factors that bring about dissension and discord in our contemporary, post–Cold War world, and then identify positive and constructive non-violent actions that Conscientious Objector nations might take to mitigate and eliminate these negatives. For example, a focus on the issues of poverty, over-population, over-consumption by the rich nations, religious and ethnic differences, environmental disasters, resource depletion, unequal and unjust social and economic development, lack of meaningful employment, youth boredom and alienation,

非暴力についての近年の偉大な理論家でもあり実践家でもあったモハンダス・K・ガンジー（通称マハトマ）について一言するなら、正義とともなう平和を求めるにあたり、「真理」と「非暴力」とを綯い交ぜるという彼のサチャグラハ哲学と実践とをよりよく理解するとすれば、それはわれわれのプラスとなってくれるかも知れない。[3]

　ガンジーの説く意味において、われわれは普遍性をもつ真理たる憲法9条から力を得、断固としてしかも非暴力の力をもって、この真理こそ日本やそれ以外の国々によっても尊重されてしかるべきであると主張できよう。

　またわれわれは故マーチン・ルーサー・キング牧師の努力に徴することもできよう。彼こそはガンジーの理論と実践を援用かつ精緻化し、アメリカ黒人の平等ならびに尊厳をともなう正義とを求める戦いに適用してみせたのである。

　長期にわたり非暴力の紛争解決を研究し実践してきたジーネ・シャープは彼の3巻ものの著作の中巻で、非暴力の抗議運動ならびに説得の具体的な方法を198通りも紹介している。[4]

　ここでCO国家が軍務に代わって実践しうる代替奉仕サービスの種類を短く列挙し、それについて敷衍することにする。

CO国家のための代替奉仕サービス

　CO国家は次のような形において代替奉仕サービスを実践することができよう。

1. 予防外交など戦争防止の諸形式についての実験と実践を試みる。
2. 人口増加を押さえる。

and international weapons trade—all suggest a multitude of non-violent actions that might be taken by CO nations.

Mohandas K. Gandhi, one of the greatest recent theorists and practitioners of non-violence, might help us if we can better understand his *Satyagraha* philosophy and practice of blending "truth" and "non-violence" in seeking peace with justice.[3] In a Gandhian sense, we might draw strength from the universal Article 9 truth and, with firmness and non-violent force, insist that this truth be honored by Japan and by the other nations.

We might draw from the efforts of the late Martin Luther King, Jr., who applied extensions and refinements of Gandhi's theory and practice to black people's struggles in America for equality and justice with dignity.

Gene Sharp, a long-time student and practitioner of non-violent means of conflict resolution has outlined 198 specific methods of non-violent protest and persuasion in volume two of his three volume set of books.[4]

Let me now elaborate on the short list of kinds of alternative service that might be carried out by Conscientious Objector nations in lieu of military service.

Alternative Service For Conscientious Objector Nations

Conscientious Objector nations might perform alternative national service by (1) experimenting with and practicing preventive diplomacy and other forms of war prevention. They might work to (2) reduce population growth; (3) assist sustainable social and economic development; (4) overcome

3. 持続可能な社会・経済開発を助ける。

4. 世界飢餓と貧困を克服する。

5. 巨大な難民問題に対処する。

6. 人権抑圧の発生を減らす。

7. 核兵器の貯蔵量をゼロに減らす。

8. 通常兵器の輸出入による移転を止める。

9. 非暴力行動と紛争解決の啓蒙を行う。

10. 自己防衛にあたっては、ジーネ・シャープがその『市民ベース防衛：脱軍事用武器システム』[5]で明かしているようなシステムを使う。

11. 天然資源を保護保存し、環境破壊を少なくし、GTBDを設計、製造、マーケティングしていく。

1. 予防外交と戦争防止

　戦争放棄を法律で定めた憲法9条をもつ日本は、国連憲章第4章「紛争の平和的処理」第33条にうたわれた非暴力的手段を用いることで、予防外交や戦争防止の面で世界規模でのリーダーシップをとれる恰好な立場にある。これらの手段には「交渉、調査、調停、和解、斡旋、司法解決、地域の諸機関や取り決め、ほか紛争当事者の選ぶ平和的な手段に訴えての解決」などが含まれる。[6]日本が改組された国連において常任安保理事国の椅子を占めた暁には、国連憲章の第33条こそが、世界平和と公正への日本の主たる責任と貢献になるものと思われる。

　予防外交、戦争防止、非暴力的な紛争解決などの分野での最近の希望のもてる実例としては、パレスチナとイスラエルとが殺戮しあう代わりに話し合うことに決まる上でのノル

world hunger and poverty; (5) cope with massive refugee problems; (6) reduce human rights violations; (7) reduce nuclear arsenals to zero; (8) stop international trade in conventional weapons; (9) educate for non-violent action and conflict resolution; and (10) defend themselves with Civilian Based Defense (CBD) as outlined by Gene Sharp in his book, *Civilian-Based Defense: A Post-Military Weapons System*[5]; (11) preserve and conserve natural resources, reduce environmental degradation, design manufacture and market "green technology by design."

1. Preventive Diplomacy and War Prevention

Japan with its Article 9 legal injunction against war is in a position to provide world-class leadership in preventive diplomacy and war prevention using the non-violent methods suggested in the Charter of the United Nations, Chapter VI, "Pacific Settlement of Disputes," Article 33. These include seeking solutions "... by negotiation, enquiry, mediation, conciliation, arbitration, judicial settlement, resort to regional agencies or arrangements, or other peaceful means of ..." the disputants' own choice.[6] In fact, when Japan becomes a permanent member of the UN Security Council in a reorganized United Nations, Article 33 of the UN Charter might well be one of Japan's major responsibilities and contributions for world peace and justice.

Recent encouraging examples of preventive diplomacy, war prevention, and non-violent conflict resolution include Norwegian efforts to bring Palestinian and Israeli people to talk

ウェーの介在、新しい南アフリカ政府の変身、ジミー・カーター元米大統領による朝鮮半島での核問題への非政府レベルでのかかわりに加えハイチその他での彼の業績、それにクリントン政権による旧ユーゴスラビヤでの相対立するグループ間での和平斡旋の努力、などをあげることができる。不幸なことだが、ユーゴ情勢にまつわる矛盾は、一方でアメリカがボスニアのイスラム教徒を訓練し装備するなど軍事中心主義を反映している側面がつよいのに、他方では和平安定軍とともに殺戮に終止符を打とうとしているという点にある。

　一般日本人であれ指導者であれ、国際的な平和維持活動に兵士を送らないことに対し、肩身を狭くし悪びれる必要はさらさらない。平和憲法と憲法9条を堂々と尊重し、予防外交、戦争防止、それに代替奉仕の諸面で先頭に立つことで、日本は次の一千年期を前に、緊急に求められしかも、ずうっと高次で原則度の高い模範を示すことができる。

2. 人口増加

　日本が着実に憲法9条の精神を回復していくにともない、世界平和と公正とになしうるもっとも顕著な非暴力的な貢献の1つは、世界人口の伸びに待ったをかけることであろう。軍事面の削減によって生じる人材や、経済や、物質面での節約の一部を、人口抑制、家族計画、両性の啓蒙、継続可能な社会経済開発などに振り向けることで、国連であれ他の平和維持活動であれ兵士を派遣するよりは、平和と公正へのはるかに大きな貢献が可能となる。

　人間の悲惨、紛争、地球温暖化それに生態系の破壊に連なるもっとも基本的な駆動力は人口の増加である。劫初以来、

with, rather than kill, one another; the metamorphosis of the new South African government; the talking rather than killing in Northern Ireland; former President Jimmy Carter's recent non-governmental involvement with the nuclear issue in Korea and his work in Haiti and elsewhere; and the Clinton administration's attempts to mediate peace between the warring factions in the former Yugoslavia. Unfortunately, the Yugoslavian situation too much reflects a militarist perspective with the US training and arming the Bosnian Muslims while at the same time trying to stop the killing with the Implementation Force.

Never should the Japanese people or their leaders feel guilty for not sending soldiers on international peace-keeping operations. By proudly honoring their peace constitution and Article 9, with leadership in preventive diplomacy, war prevention, and other forms of alternative service, Japan can demonstrate an urgently needed and much higher and more principled path as a model for the new millennium.

2. Population Growth

As Japan steadily restores the integrity of Article 9, one of the most significant non-violent contributions for world peace and justice it might make would be to encourage world population reduction. Shifting some of the human, financial, and material resources saved from the military to worldwide population control, family planning, women's and men's education, sustainable social and economic development would make a far greater contribution to peace and justice than sending soldiers on UN or other peace-keeping operations.

Population growth is one of the fundamental driving forces leading to human suffering, conflict, global warming,

スラムには、雨滴をしのぐだけの粗末な家がどこまでも続く。（ペルー）

In the slums, flimsy houses capable of no more than keeping out the rain stretch to the horizon. (Peru)

1830年に世界人口が10億人に達するのに、実に100万年以上を要した。が、次の10億人が増えるのには1930年までに100年しか要さなかった。そしてその後60年経った1990年までの間に50億人に達した。紀元2001年までには、もし増加率がいまのままだとすれば、60億人になる。[7]マイケル・トビヤスは、野放しにされた人間の出生率をガンに喩え、苦痛や悲惨、死や生物圏の破壊につながる、と記している。[8]

人口削減は宗教・民族次元の信条や慣行によって複雑の度を加える。この制約は日本よりはアメリカにおける方が問題かも知れぬ。1980年代から1990年代の初頭に至り、レーガン・ブッシュ両政権は保守派の政治上宗教上の懸念につきうごかされ、世界規模での家族計画活動への経済援助を打ち切った。信じがたいことながら当時の政府有力者は地球にとって人口抑制などは不要とのたもうた。のみならず、人口は多々ますます弁ず、などと主張したのだった。恐らく日本にあってはこの手の国内政治上の困難は存在せず、先進国と途上国の双方における人口削減について世界を先導していく上に支障はないのではなかろうか。

3. 持続可能な社会・経済開発

CO国家としての日本の平和と公正ならびに環境と折り合っていく上での最大の貢献は、途上国を援助し、彼らをして人権尊重と緑のテクノロジーの諸原則に見合った形で、しかも憲法9条の非暴力・非軍事という原則の尊重の上に立って、その生活水準の向上をはかっていくことを助勢する点にあろう。

and other ecosystem destruction. It took from the dawn of humanity until 1830, over a million years, for world population to reach one billion people. The second billion took only one hundred years, from 1830 to 1930. By 1990, sixty years later, world population had grown to five billion. In the year 2001 it will be six billion if rates of population growth are not reduced.[7] Writer Michael Tobias speaks of uncontrolled human fertility as being like a cancer that leads to pain, misery, death and biosphere destruction.[8]

Population reduction is complicated by religious and ethnic beliefs and practices, constraints that might be less of a problem for Japan than for the USA. Reagan and Bush administration policies in the 1980s and early 1990s, driven by conservative political-religious concerns, brought about the termination of US funding for worldwide family planning. Unbelievably, influential persons in government during those years argued that the world need not control population growth. In fact they argued that the more people the better. Presumably Japan would not have these kinds of domestic political difficulties in providing world-class leadership for population reductions in both developed and developing nations.

3. Sustainable Social and Economic Development

Some of Japan's most significant conscientious objector contributions for peace and justice, and for peace with the environment, can come from assistance to developing nations that enables them to improve living standards in ways that are compatible with the best human rights and green technology principles, and which honor the non-violent, non-military principles of Article 9.

日本のODA憲章の基本的な理念と原則とは、前出の数パラグラフに盛られた考え方と平仄（ひょうそく）を合わせている。[9] 日本は途上国に人道的な経済開発援助を基本的な人権と自由とを確保するような、環境的に健全な形で、しかも市場経済の文脈の中で提供しようとしている。ODAの資金が軍事目的に用いられたり、被援助国によって兵器の輸出入に使われることは、これを明示的にいましめている。

　ODAの4大原則とは

1. 環境保全と開発とは両々相俟った形で追い求められねばならない。

2. ODA資金を軍事目的ないしは国際紛争の激化のために使うことは避けられるべきである。

3. 被援助国による軍事支出の趨勢、大量破壊兵器やミサイル類の開発や生産、輸出入を通しての武器の移転などに対しては十全な注意が払われねばならない。これは国際平和と安定との維持強化のためであり、途上国はその資源の配分にあたっては自国の経済的社会的発展にしかるべき優先順位を付すべきである、という見地からである。

4. 民主化と市場志向経済の導入の促進、ならびに基本的人権と諸自由の確保のための努力に対し十全な注意が払われなければならない。

　日本はそのODA計画を通じ、すでに絶対額では世界最大の供与国（ドーナー）である。1993年には112.6億ドル、[11] 94年には132.4億ドル[10]を提供しており、アメリカの97.2億ドル（93年）と対比される。

　但し対GNP比、となると日本もアメリカもデンマークやノ

Japan's Official Development Assistance (ODA) Charter's basic philosophy and principles sound like the ideas in the paragraph above. Japan seeks to provide humanitarian economic development assistance for developing nations in an environmentally healthy way that secures basic human rights and freedoms within the context of market-oriented economic principles. It specifically seeks to keep ODA funds from being used in any way for military purposes or the production and export or import of weapons by the recipient country. ODA's four guiding principles are:

1. Environmental conservation and development should be pursued in tandem.

2. Any use of ODA for military purposes or for aggravation of international conflicts should be avoided.

3. Full attention should be paid to trends in recipient countries' military expenditures, their development and production of mass destruction weapons and missiles, their export and import of arms, etc., so as to maintain and strengthen international peace and stability, and from the viewpoint that developing countries should place appropriate priorities in the allocation of their resources on their own economic and social development.

4. Full attention should be paid to efforts for promoting democratization and introduction of a market-oriented economy, and the situation regarding the securing of basic human rights and freedoms in the recipient country.

Japan, through its ODA programs, is already the world's largest donor in absolute magnitude—a total of $13.24 billion in 1994[10] and $11.26 billion in 1993.[11] The USA contributed $9.72 billion in 1993. As a percentage of Gross National Product (GNP) neither Japan nor the USA come close to the

ルウェー、スウェーデンやオランダのような欧州諸国には遠く及ばない。具体的にいうなら、1993年に日本のODA拠出高はGNPの0.26%（アメリカは0.15%）であったのに比し、デンマークとノルウェー、スウェーデンとオランダとはそれぞれ、1.03%、1.01%、0.98%、0.8%を記録した。[12] 非軍事面でのアメリカの対外援助は、さらに削減の可能性に見舞われているが、反対に軍事援助——日本のODA計画では禁じられている——は結構をきわめる繁昌ぶりである。

　平和維持活動に対し兵士を送っていないではないかと批判された際には、憲法9条に縛られているのでなどと悪びれる代わりに、平和と公正とのコストの負担分として、ODAを通じもっと意味のある非暴力的な貢献をこのように行っているという点を、世界に周知させる上での絶好の機会と捉えるべきである。

　アメリカのAID（国際協力庁）などの開発援助計画が問題をかかえているのと同様、日本のODA計画にも数多くの問題点が存在する。これらは正されねばならないし、新しいビジョンが創られ実行に移されねばならない。これらの問題点のうちより顕著な1つは、開発援助計画が往々にして自利を目的としている、という点である。つまりは、主たる目的が、援助供与国自体を助けることにあるのではないかと見える点である。被援助国をそっちのけにして、である。現にアメリカにおいては、開発援助資金の用途は、しばしばアメリカの技術や専門知識の買い付けに限られている。この欠陥を乗り越える1つの方法は、援助に当たっては定評のあるしかるべき国際もしくは1国の非政府組織を通じ、ヒモの付かない形で行う、ということであろう。

　日本のODAの対GNP比がさらに増大して、スカンジナヴィア諸国のそれと拮抗、さらには凌駕するようになったとしたら、平和と公正への日本の貢献がもっと積極的で前向きなものになるのに、と思うことはわれわれをワクワクさせる。

commitment of many European countries such as Denmark, Norway, Sweden and the Netherlands. To illustrate, in 1993 Japan contributed 0.26 percent of its GNP as official development assistance, the USA 0.15 percent, Denmark 1.03, Norway 1.01, Sweden 0.98, and the Netherlands 0.8.[12] Non-military foreign aid by America is presently threatened with further cuts while US military assistance, which Japan's ODA program prohibits, is a thriving enterprise for the USA.

When criticized by others for not sending soldiers on peace-keeping missions—rather than apologize for being constrained by Article 9—Japan should seize the opportunity to let the world know that it is making a much more significant non-violent contribution to peace and justice through its ODA programs, as its share of the costs for peace and justice.

There are many problems with Japan's ODA as there are with America's Agency for International Development and other development assistance programs. These need to be corrected and new visions must be created and implemented. One of the more significant of these problems is the fact that development assistance activities are often self-serving—that is, a primary goal seems to be that of assisting the donor country more than the receiving one. In America, money for development assistance frequently must be used to buy technology and expertise only from the US. One way to overcome this flaw would be to channel help, with no strings attached, through recognized reputable international and national non-governmental organizations.

It is exciting to contemplate the even greater positive contributions for peace and justice that Japan could make were its ODA efforts to be further amplified to match and surpass the percentage contributions of the Scandinavian coun-

スモーキー・マウンテンで働くほとんどの人たちは、都会に憧れ、田舎から出てきた。（フィリピン、マニラ）

The people who work on Smoky Mountain were lured from the countryside by the attractions of city life. (Manila, Philippines)

自衛隊への予算を着実に減らしていくことで、このための経費を大幅にまかなうことが可能となろう。とくに大事なのは、このようにして使途が自由になった資金の一部を、環境的にクリーンで経済社会開発を助ける上に必要な技能の訓練や教育を日本の有為な若者に施すためにふり向ける、ということであろう。若者の理想主義やエネルギーに火をつけるようなこれらの有意義な仕事は、日本の若者に軍事的な仕事の常としての人殺しや破壊への訓練を施すよりは、どれほど健全か、計り知れない。

4. 世界の飢餓と貧困

　世界の飢餓と貧困との問題は人口削減と持続可能な社会・経済開発と密接に結びついている。

　第1世界の国々はその開発援助を実施するに際し、環境を痛めつけず、環境空間と地球の資源とをより公正に頒ちあっていくことのできるような、健全な社会経済開発を刺戟することに重点をおかなければならない。日本が自衛隊用の支出を減らすにともなって、この種の目的に重点をおいたODAを拡大し、意味のある仕事向けに日本の若者を訓練することで、世界に範を垂れることができる。

5. 難民問題

　紛争や暴力は世界を覆いつくし、ほんの数例だが、ルアンダからボスニアからアフガニスタンに至る全世界で何百万人という難民が生み出されている。憲法9条の諸原則や紛争解決のための非暴力的な手段が支配する世界ができるまでの間は、難民という立場に追いやられた人類の仲間のための、人道的な援助の必要は急を要する。人間的な紛争を非暴力的に

tries. A steadily shrinking Self-Defense Forces budget could provide much of this additional funding. Especially important would be to use some of those liberated funds to educate and train significant numbers of Japan's brightest and best young people in the skills needed to assist environmentally clean social and economic development. These worthwhile jobs, ones that might truly tap youthful idealism and energy, would be so much more healthy than training Japan's youth for killing and destruction—the essence of military jobs.

4. World Hunger and Poverty

World hunger and poverty are intimately related to population reduction and sustainable social and economic development. First-world nations must focus their development assistance so as to stimulate healthy social and economic development that does not desecrate the environment, and which ultimately leads to a more equitable sharing of environmental space and the Earth's resource base. Japan, as it reduces SDF spending, can set an example by expanding its ODA with a focus on these objectives and by educating and training Japanese youth for these meaningful kinds of work.

5. Refugee Problems

Conflicts and violence abound all around the globe leaving millions of refugees from Rwanda to Bosnia to Afghanistan —to name but a few. Until we attain a world dominated by Article 9 principles and non-violent means for conflict resolution, there is urgent need for humanitarian assistance to those sisters and brothers who are afflicted with refugee sta-

解決することをついに身につけたあとといえども、自然の猛威からの難民、たとえば地震や台風などの被害者は残る。

　CO国家としての日本がこの種の罹災者を助けるための特別な緊急グループを教育し訓練することは重要である。軍隊の1つの効用はこの点にある、という論を成す向きもある。が、残念ながら殺人と破壊のための軍事的な訓練は、難民救助にとっては不向きでしかない。軍隊とは無関係な特別緊急対処グループが必要とされるのである。

　日本が改組された国連安保理事会の常任理事国になったときに、CO国家としての日本ができる平和と公正への非暴力的な貢献の最たるものの1つは、国連難民担当弁務官というポストをより一層重みのあるものにする上に、さらなるリーダーシップを示すことであろう。

6. 人権侵害

　人権侵害事件は世界に充ち満ちている。そのODA援助や他の関連する諸機関のもてるものの大きな部分を、人権侵害の縮小に向け、各地域における、また各国政府による人間への取り扱い方を改善する上に資していけたとすれば、憲法9条を尊重するこれ以上の方法が果たしてありうるだろうか。難民の場合と同じく、日本は国連を通じ、とくに国連人権機構とその傘下の人権委員会を通じ、人権問題についての国連の活動を強化する上でのリーダーシップをふるうことができるであろう。

　憲法9条に催された誇り高きCO国家として、紛争解決のためのさまざまな非暴力的手段で指導的な立場に立つ日本は、全世界の人権侵害を減らしていく上で大きな前向きの影響を

tus. Even when we finally learn to resolve our human conflicts non-violently, we will still have refugees from nature's violence—earthquakes, typhoons, etc. It is important that Japan, as a Conscientious Objector nation, educate and train special rapid response groups to assist those in need. Some would argue that this is one way to utilize military personnel. Unfortunately, military training for killing and destruction is inappropriate training for helping refugees. Special rapid response groups with no military connection are necessary.

Perhaps when Japan becomes a permanent member of the reorganized UN Security Council, one of its significant non-violent contributions to peace and justice as a Conscientious Objector nation could be to provide additional leadership so as to further elevate the office of the UN High Commissioner for Refugees.

6. Human Rights Violations

Human rights abuses abound around the globe. What better way for Japan to honor its Article 9 than to devote a significant portion of its ODA and other related agency resources to reducing human rights violations, and encouraging improvements in the ways that people are treated in their societies and by their governments. As with refugees, Japan, through the UN, might provide additional leadership for strengthening UN activities for human rights through the UN Commission on Human Rights and its Human Rights Committee, and in other ways.

By being a proud Article 9-driven Conscientious Objector nation, and leading in a multiplicity of ways with non-violent means for conflict resolution, Japan can have a very

奴隷同然の生活を強いられていた
ハイチ人の家族。現在でも、全世
界に2億人の奴隷がいると報じられ
ている。（ドミニカ）

A family of people who have been
forced to lives of virtual slavery.
There are said to be 200,000,000
slaves in the world even now.
(Dominica)

与えていくことができる。何はともあれ、すべての人間の権利のうちもっとも基本的なものは、近代的なハイテク戦争にまつわる無差別な暴虐の手で、焼却されたり、蒸発させられたり、放射能を浴びせかけられたりしないで済む、という権利だからである。

7. 核兵器の蓄積

　核兵器によって焼却され、蒸発させられ、放射能を浴びた地球上の唯一無二の体験者としての日本が、この破滅的な兵器の廃絶を目指す戦いの先頭に立つ資格を手にしていることは間違いない。米ソ対立の被害妄想が終わりを告げた今日だけに、日本がアメリカの核の傘なるものから脱け出し、広島長崎の瓦礫から作られ憲法9条と平和憲法とに装おられた、日本独自の傘を自らにさしかける時が到来した、といえるのではないか。このことは世界平和に対する日本の最大な貢献になるべく運命づけられている。日本国民はすべからく自国の指導者に、この問題についての唯一のまっとうなリーダーシップのあり方として核兵器ゼロ路線を進めていくよう、つよく主張すべきである。

　核兵器廃棄を全世界の多くの人々が訴えてきた。日本でこの目標を求めてきた人士の中にはノーベル賞受賞の、故湯川秀樹博士をはじめ故木村一治教授や豊田利幸教授のような著名な物理学者が含まれている。[13, 14] 1つ皮肉なのはこれらの物理学者に、最近アメリカ戦略空軍の前司令官、リー・バトラー退役大将（第2章に既出）が加わったことであり、同大将の見解に賛意を表し共同署名した、退役将軍60人ほどのうちの2人は、左近允尚敏元統幕会議事務局長と志方俊之元陸自北部方面総監という日本人だということである。

positive impact on reducing human rights abuses all around the globe. After all, one of the most fundamental of all human rights is the right not to have oneself incinerated, vaporized, or irradiated by the indiscriminate brutality of modern high-technology warfare.

7. Nuclear Arsenals

As the only people on Earth to have been evaporated, irradiated, and incinerated with nuclear weapons, there is no question but that Japan has earned the right to lead the fight to eliminate holocaust weapons. Now that USA–USSR Cold War paranoia has ended, perhaps it is time for Japan to step out from under the USA's nuclear umbrella and carry its own. Japan's umbrella, fashioned out of Hiroshima and Nagasaki ashes and clothed with the Peace Constitution and Article 9, is destined to be one of Japan's most significant contributions for world peace. Japanese people must insist that their leaders pursue a zero nuclear weapons path as the only appropriate world-class leadership on this issue.

Many around the world have long been calling for the elimination of nuclear weapons. Among those in Japan seeking this goal have been distinguished Japanese physicists, the late Nobel laureate Hideki Yukawa, the late Motoharu Kimura, and Toshiyuki Toyoda.[13, 14] It is ironic that this group of physicists has recently been joined by the former commander of the US Strategic Air Command, retired General Lee Butler (as noted in chapter 2), and that among some sixty retired admirals and generals concurring with him two were from Japan (retired Vice Admiral Naotoshi Sakonjo and retired Lt. General Toshiyuki Shikata).

厳寒から身を守るために作られた
土壁の家。それに用いられた黄色
い土に放射能が含まれていた。こ
の家の長男は脳と身体に重い障害
をもって生まれた。(シベリア、
ウラン鉱山近くの村)

This house is built with thick mud
walls for protection against the
winter cold. But the yellow earth
contained radioactive material.
The older son in the family was
born with severe brain damage and
other physical impediments. (Vil-
lage near a uranium mine, Siberia)

1980年代の半ば、当時ニュージーランドの首相だったデビッド・ロンギは、核搭載のアメリカ艦船の同国港湾への入港を拒否し、非核地帯路線をとることで時のレーガン米政権と決別した。[15] アメリカ側は通商制限などさまざまな威迫を行ったが、ロンギは自国からアメリカの核兵器をしめ出すことに成功、非核ニュージーランドを作り上げたのである。

　世界から核兵器をとり除くという作業の先頭に立つという役割を果たすにあたり、日本はその非核3原則（持たない・作らない・持ち込ませない）を検討しなおし、ニュージーランドと同じく、非核日本になるべきであろう。将来の日米間の安全保障論議にあっては、非核地帯という発想がその一部分になっていかねばならない。

　1995年11月、バンコックにおいて、アセアン諸国は東南アジア非核地帯の設置に関する条約に署名した。[16] 域内の通商活動を促進する、という取り決めと同時にである。たしかに核保有の5大国への規制に関するかぎり抜け穴だらけである。とはいえ、その伝達する意味合いは強烈だった。核兵器のような没義道な「おもちゃ」なんぞみなお蔵にしたかったのである。アメリカ、中国それにフランスの3核保有国はこの非核地帯条約には不満で、バンコック会議で賛成を拒否した。[17]

　中国とフランスとは、1996年の包括核実験停止条約の発効前夜に、核実験を再開することでその無責任ぶりを示した。フランスは傲岸不遜にも自国周辺の環境を汚染することには気が進まぬが、遠く地球を半周した南太平洋のムルロア環礁での実験には心を痛めることはなかった。フランスと中国による核実験の再開も、アメリカに部分的にであれ追いつきたいとする希求のあらわれとして判らないでもない。

In the mid 1980s New Zealand Prime Minister David Lange steered a Nuclear Free course with which he alienated the Reagan administration by refusing to allow nuclear armed vessels into New Zealand's harbors.[15] While there was much huffing and puffing about trade restrictions and other threats made by the United States, Lange was successful in keeping US nuclear weapons out of New Zealand. He established a Nuclear-Free New Zealand. Perhaps in its leadership role in ridding the world of these weapons, Japan should review its own three non-nuclear principles (not possessing, not manufacturing, and not permitting the entry of nuclear weapons) and do the same as did New Zealand—become a Nuclear-Free Japan. The idea of nuclear-free zones needs to become a part of discussions between Japan and the USA in future security agreement negotiations.

In November, 1995, in Bangkok, the Association of Southeast Asian Nations signed the Southeast Asian Nuclear Weapons Free Zone treaty along with an agreement to promote trade within the region.[16] Even though this treaty is full of holes relative to constraining the "nuclear five," it sends a strong message. People want those immoral "toys" put away. The USA, China, and France were unhappy with this nuclear-free-zone treaty and declined to back it at the Bangkok meeting.[17]

Both China and France have recently demonstrated irresponsibility in renewed nuclear testing on the eve of a 1996 comprehensive nuclear weapons test ban treaty. France, in its arrogance, is unwilling to pollute its own environment, but is quite comfortable in doing so halfway around the world, on Mururoa Atoll in the South Pacific. This new round of nuclear testing by France and China is perhaps understand-

すでに多くの実験データを手にしているアメリカは、コンピューターによるシミュレーションのソフトを開発しおわっており、もはや現場でのリアルタイムの実験は、核兵器の設計や製造にとって不可欠ではなくなっているのである。[18]

　日本の市民も自国の指導者に対し、日本の経済力、憲法9条の道義性、広島長崎を経験したことの迫力を綯い交ぜて、核実験停止からさらに一歩を進め、全世界の核兵器の廃絶に向かうよう、勇気づけていくべきである。

　一方、日本国民も指導者も、この分野で先頭に立つ資格を自らの苦難を経てかちとったことをしっかりと見てとり、核兵器の山をゼロに減らすために堂々かつ決然と前進していくよう力づけられねばならない。この代替奉仕サービスを遂行していくにあたり、日本は世界平和と公正のためのもっとも有意義な非暴力の貢献の1つとして、これらの活動を全世界に向かって宣言し周知せしめていってしかるべきである。

8. 国際的な武器取り引き

　憲法9条のおかげも手伝って、国際的な武器取り引きへの日本の参加は、最小限にとどまっている。かつてのソ連邦が解体した今日においては、通常兵器の移転取り引きで他国をグンと引き離しているのは、アメリカである。

　1993年のアメリカ議会調査局の報告によると、途上国への通商兵器の最大の輸出国はアメリカで、世界のこの市場のおそよ73%を占めている。[19] 1994年、この不名誉きわまりない首位を占めたのは、どうやらフランスであった。クリントン政権の商務長官ならびに通商代表は、この唾棄すべき通商高の増大に献身しているように見える。わが国の兵器製造工場に生産活動の歯車をまわさせつづけ、その株主に配当を与えつづけ、何百何千万人ものアメリカ市民に職場を提供しつづけるためにである。

able in that they seek to partially catch up with the United States. With its reams of test data, the USA has developed computer simulation software so that real-time actual tests are no longer an essential for designing and building nuclear devices.[18]

Japanese citizens must encourage their leaders to bring Japan's economic power, its Article 9's moral power, and its Hiroshima and Nagasaki experiential power to the task of moving beyond a nuclear test ban treaty to the abolition of nuclear weapons everywhere. Japanese people and their leaders must be encouraged to clearly recognize their earned right to lead in this arena, and to then move ahead with dignity and resolve to reduce nuclear arsenals to zero. As Japan carries out this alternative service it should proclaim and publicize these efforts worldwide, as one of its most significant non-violent contributions for world peace and justice.

8. International Weapons Trade

Thanks in part to Article 9, Japan participates minimally in the international arms trade. Now that the USSR is gone, the USA by far leads the world in conventional weapons trade. A 1993 US Congressional Research Service report lists the USA as the world's leading exporter of conventional weapons to developing countries—accounting for some 73 percent of this world market.[19] Apparently, this dishonorable first place became France's for 1994. The US Department of Commerce and the Trade Representative in the Clinton administration seem quite dedicated to increasing this species of abominable trade as a way to keep our weapons factories buzzing and profitable for stockholders, and in providing work for millions of American citizens.

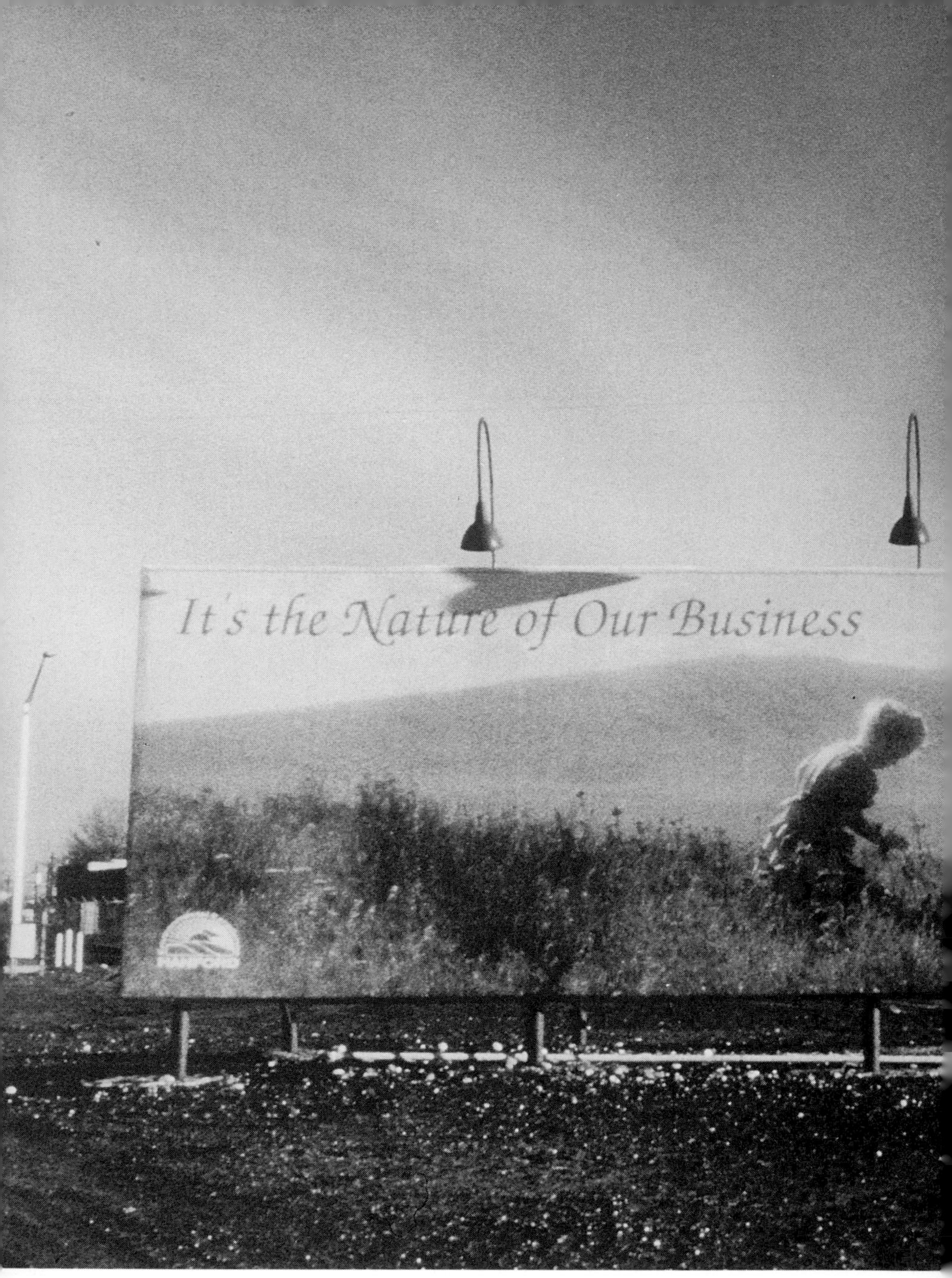
It's the Nature of Our Business

施設入り口の看板。子どもたちの上には「これが私たちの本質です」の文字。背後にあるのは核研究施設。（アメリカ、ハンフォード）

A large billboard at the entrance to a nuclear complex. Above the children it reads, "It is the Nature of Our Business." In the background can be seen the nuclear research center. (Hanford, Washington)

これからの通商交渉においては、日本側の交渉者たるもの、自国が武器取り引きを控えているという事実をテコとして、アメリカが世界最大の武器セールスマンであることを思いとどまるよう、強力に訴えてはと思う。日米2国間の通商問題の一部を、アメリカの武器通商取り引きという麻薬からの治療を助けるような創造的な解毒促進計画と組み合わせることが可能であろう。

　武器取り引きを減らす上で日本がより積極的な主導的な立場をとるに当たっては、全世界に対しそのことを宣言、周知させていくことも欠かせない。

9. 非暴力活動と紛争解決

　世界が今日暴力的な軍事手段に使っている金額は年間、1兆ドルに上り、それは1分間に200万ドルにもあたる。[20] こんな手段があっても、長い目でみるならば、お互いの間の対立を消す上に役立ちはしない。過去の戦争の結果に対する経費の支払いを含むなら、軍事面での支出は、もっと大きな規模に達する。ところが世界ときたら、非暴力的な紛争解決のための援助や教育には、ビタ1文も出していないのに等しい。日本がもし自衛隊予算の僅か5％をさっぴいて、その金額を世界各地で使って、お互い同士の不一致を非暴力的に解決していくための、社会の各段階における啓蒙教育や訓練に充当したとするならば、世界平和や公正にとってどれほどすばらしい貢献になるか、想像してみよう。

10. 市民ベースの防衛

　争いは人間存在と不可分、という認識の上に立つジーネ・シャープは、非暴力の争闘についての幅広い知識に依拠して、武器をとっての紛争に取って代わりうるのは何かを明らかに

I would hope that in future trade talks, Japanese negotiators might use Japan's demonstration of restraint in international weapons trade to strongly urge the USA to stop being the world's top weapons sales agent. Perhaps some of the bilateral trade issues between Japan and the US could be linked to a creative detoxification program that might gradually help cure America's international weapons sales addiction.

As Japan moves to more aggressively demonstrate international leadership in reducing weapons trade, it should also proclaim and publicize this effort to its citizens and to the world.

9. Educate For Non-Violent Action and Conflict Resolution

The world presently spends close to a trillion dollars per year, about two million dollars per minute, on violent military means.[20] These are means that in the long run really do not help us settle our differences. If we include continuing expenditures for the consequences of past wars, these annual military costs are very much higher. Yet the world spends practically nothing on helping and educating us for non-violent conflict resolution. Imagine what a wonderful contribution for world peace and justice Japan could make if it were to take but 5 percent of its SDF budget and spend it around the world on education and training at all levels of society in non-violent means for settling our differences.

10. Civilian-Based Defense

Recognizing that conflict is a part of the human condition, Gene Sharp draws on his extensive studies of non-violent struggle to develop an alternative to armed conflict. He

してみせた。一般市民が大々的かつ対象を選んで非協力や鼻先であしらう姿勢をつらぬきさえすれば、近代的なハイテク戦争の危険に会うことなく、相手方の侵略者の目的達成をはばむことができることを明かしてみせた。

彼はいう。

　　市民ベース（CBD）の防衛とは、非暴力行動ないしは非暴力闘争の一般的な手法を、精緻かつ高度な形で、国防の問題に応用したものである。……市民ベースの防衛は一般市民とその組織が、高度な準備、計画、それに訓練の上に立って展開されるべきものとされる。……市民ベースの防衛とは、政治権力とはそれが国内に由来すると外国に由来するとにかかわらず、それぞれの社会内部にその源泉をもつという理論の上に成り立っている。これらの力の源泉を認めないか断ち切りさえすれば、一般市民が統治者をコントロールし外部の侵略者を打ちまかすことだって可能となる。[21]

　この市民ベース（CBD）の防衛には多くの訓練と規律が必要とされるほか、籍すに時間をもってせねばならない。シャープは、1つの社会が従来型の軍事力による防衛からCBDに移項する過渡期のことを「脱武装」（トランスアーマメント）の時期と過程と呼んでいる。この時期と過程の間には、橋渡し作業や「脱武装」のただ中にあるかも知れない他国との信頼醸成に力めていく必要がある。

　CBDと非暴力行動とは、武器を手にしての暴力よりもより多くの勇気と放胆さとを必要とする。CBDが機能していくためには、その社会の成員がたくましく勇気をもっていなければならない。またCBDの適用にあたり、人々が全く傷つかないというわけではないが、近代戦争がもたらす修羅場と比べれば、傷つく度合いははるかに少ない。

　もしも日本が自国の世界平和への貢献の路線は非暴力の道

explains how massive and selective non-cooperation and defiance by a country's civilian population can deny aggressors their objectives without the dangers of modern high-technology war. He says:

> Civilian-based defense is an application, in a refined and developed form, of the general techniques of nonviolent action, or nonviolent struggle, to the problems of national defense. … Civilian-based defense is meant to be waged by the population and its institutions on the basis of advanced preparation, planning, and training. … Civilian-based defense rests on the theory that political power, whether of domestic or foreign origin, is derived from sources within each society. By denying or severing these sources of power, populations can control rulers and defeat foreign aggressors.[21]

CBD does not happen without a lot of training and discipline, nor does it happen overnight. Sharp speaks of the transition period when a society moves from the traditional military form of defense to CBD as the period and process of "transarmament." During this period and process there is a need to engage in bridge building, the development of trust with other nations, some of whom might also be in "transarmament."

CBD and non-violent action require more courage and bravery than does violence with weapons. In order for CBD to work, the people in a society must be strong and courageous, and though CBD also does not imply that people will not get hurt in its application, the hurt will be far less than that resulting from the carnage of modern war.

If Japan should find the will and courage to insist that its

であるべきだとする意志と勇気とを持ちあわせているなら、憲法9条の精神の全面的な復権の方向に向かって、軍事力を漸減させていくとともに、CBDに思いを馳せてしかるべきだろう。

11. 天然資源、環境破壊それにGTD

　いわゆる先進国に住んでいるのは地球全人口の5分の1だが、この人たちが全資源の80%近くを消費しているのに、残りの5分の4の途上国の住民は、地球というこのホシの善きものの残りの20%を消費することをお情けで許されているにすぎない。途上世界の住民は豊かな国々でのたっぷりとした消費を目にして、物質的な消費こそが幸福と満足との鍵であると誤認しがちである。そこで消費ゲームに参加しようと望むことも自然な勢いである。10年ほど前に私は仕事で中国に住んでいたのだが、ほとんどの中国人は、車を1台は持ちたいと望み、その上近代的なマーケティング手法を通してたえず見せつけられる一方の物質的な善きものの一切を手にしたいと思っていた。豊かな国に住んでいるお互いが、自分たちを突き動かしているのと同じ物質的豊かさを彼らには拒む権利など果たしてあるだろうか。

　われわれが生物の種として直面している問題を一口でいうなら、人口と経済成長がたえず伸びつづけているというのに、空間と資源には限りがあり、増えつづける一方のゴミの流れを処理するにも処理場の数は限られている、という点である。[22, 23, 24]冷戦が終わった今日にあっては、全世界が自由な市場資本主義という列車に乗りこむのに懸命で、成長と物質的消費とがすべてを束ねているかすがい、という調子である。
　経済成長こそは市民によりよい生活を可能にする魔法の杖、というのが各国の見方となった。ただ以下で見るように、

path for world peace be the road of non-violent contribution, then as it gradually moves toward a restoration of the full integrity of Article 9, it might well wish to consider CBD as it gradually phases out its military.

11. Natural Resources, Environmental Degradation, and "Green Technology by Design"

One fifth of Earth's people who live in developed countries consume some 80 percent of the Earth's resources while the remaining four fifths who live in less-developed nations are privileged to consume the remaining 20 percent of the planet's bounty. Those in the developing societies, noting the opulent consumption in the rich nations, are inclined to erroneously conclude that material consumption is the essential key to happiness and contentment. They thus naturally aspire to participate in this consumption game. As I learned from living and working in China a decade ago, most Chinese people would like to have a car along with all of the other material goodies they are exposed to by modern marketing methods. What right do we in the rich nations have to deny those in developing nations the same things that drive us?

The general problem that we as a species face is one of continually expanding population and economic growth in a world of finite space and resources—and of limited sinks for disposal of our growing waste streams.[22, 23, 24] Now that the Cold War has ended, the entire world seems bent on climbing on a free market capitalist railroad train with growth and material consumption as the glue to hold everything together.

Nations now see economic growth as the magic tool for enabling citizens to have a better life. Unfortunately, as we

地球上の55億人のすべてが、今日、相対的には少数派でしか
ない先進国の市民と同じ高レベルの生活様式を享受すること
は、われわれのシステムの設計や操作のやり方を大幅に変え
ぬかぎり、不可能に近い。

地球のハーフライフ

　1970年の後半、私は7年に1度の休暇を得て、連邦議会の技
術評価部門で、資源保護と汚染の問題に取り組んだ。増大す
る一方の消費と廃棄物の流れとにかかわってみて、私は地球
上のすべての人間が、いまの先進国のわれわれのように過大
な消費と環境汚染とを継続していったとして、この成長現象
なるものがどこまで引き続くものかを、訝しく思うに至った。
その答えを出すべく、私は地球のハーフライフを推定するた
めに、「工学的な試算」を行った。[25] もしも地球の全人口が
1972年のアメリカと同じ率で地球の資源を消費しはじめたと
して、一体、地球の重量の半分を使いそれを高エントロピー
の再回収不能な廃棄物に変えていくのに、どれくらいの時間
を必要とするだろうか、というのが私の自問だった。1972年
の1人あたりのアメリカ人が消費する資源——燃料ならびに
非燃料の鉱物、金属、非食料用繊維——を1日52キログラム
と試算、[26] 全地球が消費可能なしかるべき資源から成り立って
いると仮定し、人口と需要の成長率を複利で5%と仮定する
と、地球上の人間が地球の全重量の半分を消費し、高エント
ロピーの再回収不能な廃棄物に還元するのに、わずか430年
ほどしかかからない、という答えが出た。このことからはっ
きりするのは、地球上のあふれかえるような何十億人という
人々が、「豊かな」われわれと同じ高レベルの生活様式を楽
しむことは可能とは思われない。でも、これら数十億の人々
が求めているのは、まさしくこういうことなのである。

will see below, it is likely not possible for all 5.5 billion people to enjoy the same high material lifestyle that the relatively few people in the developed world enjoy—without major changes in the way we design and operate our systems.

The Half-Life of The Earth

In the late 1970s I spent a year of sabbatical leave with the US Congress Office of Technology Assessment working on resource conservation and pollution issues. This experience with ever increasing consumption and growing waste-streams stimulated me to wonder how long this growth phenomenon could go on if all humans on Earth were to over-consume and pollute as do we in the developed countries. To get an answer, I made an "engineering calculation" to estimate the half-life-of-the-Earth.[25] How long, I asked, would it take to consume half the weight of the Earth and turn it into high entropy irretrievable wastes, if Earth's entire population were to begin today to consume the Earth's resources at the same rate as did the USA in 1972? Using 1972 USA per capita consumption of resources (minerals, both fuel and non-fuel, metals, and non-food fibers) of 52 kilograms/person/day,[26] assuming that the entire globe were composed of suitably consumable materials, and assuming a 5 percent compound growth rate (population and demand), it would take only about 430 years for Earth's people to consume half the weight of the Earth and reduce it to high entropy irretrievable wastes. From this we might conclude that it is likely not possible for the teeming billions on Earth to enjoy the lifestyle of we, "the rich" —and yet that is exactly what these teeming billions seek.

巨大なブルドーザーが相手では、樹齢100年の木も1分ともたない。森が破壊されるスピードもますます加速されている。

Even a tree over 100 years old is only a minute's work for a powerful bulldozer. The destruction rate of forested land continues to accelerate.

エントロピーと経済学

　私はこの本の前段と「地球のハーフライフ」計算についての説明の中で「エントロピー」という術語を使ってきた。この複雑な熱力学上の概念を素描し、その上で、なぜ一部の経済学者が自由市場経済過程を基本的にはエントロピックなそれであるとみなしているかについて解説をこころみたい。これは、地球上の人間のすべてが先進国のお互い同様の過剰消費をすることになろうと予測しているだけにわれわれに懸念を強いてしかるべき点である。

　エントロピーというのは、熱力学の分野にあっては重要な概念である。そしてその熱力学とは、エネルギー現象を対象とする物理学や工学の一部門で、とくにエネルギーの変貌にかかわる科学的な法則が対象とされる。これらの法則の2つは、それぞれ熱力学の第1法則、第2法則と名づけられている。

　熱力学の第1法則とはエネルギー不変の法則のことで、エネルギーは新たに作られることもなければ破壊されることもない。1つの形から他の形に変容するだけで、これを高品質から低品質への変容と呼ぶ。

　熱力学の第2法則は、エネルギーの変容過程で何がおきるかを説明する上に役立つ。エネルギーが存在するのは2つの質的な状態においてである。1つは「利用可能なエネルギー」すなわち「高品質」な形で、いろいろな技術システムを動かすために使いうるエネルギーである。いま1つは、「利用不可能な」「低品質」な形のエネルギーでこれは使うことができない。エネルギーが変容するときは、ペナルティーが課せられる。ペナルティーとは、同じ種類の仕事を繰りかえす際におきる利用可能なエネルギーのロスのことで、このペナルティーを術語ではエントロピーという。

　ジェレミー・リフキンは次のように解説する。「エントロピーの増大とは、『利用可能な』エネルギーの減少を意味する。自然界にあっては何かが起きるごとに、ある量のエネル

Entropy and Economics

I have used the term "entropy" earlier in this book and in describing my "half-life-of-the-Earth" calculation. Let me offer a simplified explanation of this complex thermodynamic concept and then outline how some economists see the free-market economic process as essentially an entropic process—something that ought to concern us as we contemplate all humans on Earth over-consuming as do we in the developed countries.

Entropy is a very important concept in the field of thermodynamics, a branch of physics and engineering that deals with energy phenomena, and especially with the scientific laws which govern transformations of energy. Two of theses laws are called the First and the Second Laws of Thermodynamics.

The First Law of Thermodynamics is the same as the law of the conservation of energy. It says that energy can neither be created or destroyed. It can, however, be transformed from one form to another—from high quality to low-quality forms.

The Second Law of Thermodynamics helps to explain what happens in energy transformation processes. Energy exists in two qualitative states, (1) "available" energy, a high quality form that we can use to do work and run our various technology systems, and (2) "unavailable" energy, a low quality form that we cannot use. Every time energy is transformed, a penalty is incurred. That penalty is a loss in the amount of available energy to perform work of some kind in the future. The term for this penalty is "entropy."

Jeremy Rifkin expresses it as follows: An entropy increase, then, means a decrease in "available" energy. Every time something occurs in the natural world, some amount of

ギーは仕事の繰り返しのために利用不能で終わってしまう。
利用不能のエネルギーとは、すなわち『汚染』のことである。
多くの人々は汚染とは生産にともなう副産物だと思いこんで
いる。だが実はといえば、全世界の『利用可能』なエネルギー
のうち、『利用不能』なエネルギーへと変容させられたもの
の総和が『汚染』なのである。廃棄物というのは従ってエネ
ルギーの消退現象のことである。熱力学の第1法則によれば、
エネルギーというのは作られもせず破壊もされず、変容させ
られるだけである上に、第2法則によれば、変容の方向は一
方的、つまりは消退の方向にしか向かわない。ということに
なると、汚染というのはエントロピーの同意語といえる。つ
まりは1つのシステムに存在する、一定程度の『利用不能』
なエネルギーのことをエントロピーと呼ぶのである。」[27]

経済学者とエントロピー

　近年にいたり何人かの洞察力に富む、故ゲオルゲスク・レエー
ゲン、故ケネス・ボールディング、ハーマン・デイリー、といった
経済学者が、経済過程のもつ「エントロピック」な性格にわ
れわれの関心を喚起した。[28, 29, 30] なぜ経済過程がエントロピッ
クかというと、われわれは「高品質」（低エントロピー）の
再成不可能な資源を自然界から取り出し、それを採掘、生産、
消費し、それを「取り出し不能な廃棄物（高エントロピー）」
への処理という過程で大気や水や土地へと拡散させる。

　説明させてもらうと、ハイウェーをさんざん運転したあげ
く、自動車のタイヤを磨滅させてしまったら、「風とともに
吹き飛んでしまった」ゴムの極細な破片を拾い集め、新しい
タイヤを作る材料にすることは、物理的にも経済的にも不可
能である。タイヤを使ったことで、それを秩序ある状態から
てんでんばらばらな無秩序の状態へと追いやったわけで、つ
まりはエントロピーを増大させたということになる。

energy ends up being unavailable for future work. That unavailable energy is what pollution is all about. Many people think that pollution is a by-product of production. In fact pollution is the sum total of all of the available energy in the world that has been transformed into unavailable energy. Waste, then, is dissipated energy. Since according to the first law, energy can neither be created nor destroyed but only transformed, and since according to the second law it can only be transformed in one way—toward a dissipated state—pollution is just another name for entropy; that is, it represents a measure of the unavailable energy present in a system.[27]

Economists and Entropy

In recent times a few insightful economists such as the late Nicholas Georgescu-Roegen, the late Kenneth Boulding, and Herman Daly have sought to call our attention to the entropic nature of economic processes.[28, 29, 30] The economic process is entropic in that we extract high quality (low entropy) non-renewable resources from nature and diffuse them in extraction, production, consumption, and disposal into irretrievable waste products (high entropy) in the air, water and land. To illustrate—after we wear out automobile tires driving down the highway, it is physically and economically impossible to collect all of the minute rubber particles that have "blown in the wind" and create another tire from them. Our use of the tires has taken them from a state of order to one of randomness and disorder—an increase in entropy. Similarly, when we take virgin ores from nature,

同様に、手つかずの原鉱石を自然から取り出し、製品の旅路の果てに廃棄物処理場で地面一杯にまき散らし終わったとすれば、これらの資源は利用可能の秩序ある状態から、利用不能の、無秩序とカオスの状態に変容させられた、ということになる。

　ゲオルゲスク・レエーゲンのような非支流派の経済学者もいい、私もそれに与するものだが、貴重な天然資源という形で経済過程の中に入っていったものが、最終段階で放り出されたときは無価値の廃棄物という形をとっている、というわけである。しかし両者の質的なちがいは、やや異なるいい方であるとはいえ、熱力学という名の物理学の一分野によって実証される。熱力学の立場からすると、物質エネルギーは低エントロピーの形で経済過程に入っていき、高エントロピーの形で経済過程から出ていくのである。[31]

　経済過程とは秩序から無秩序やカオスへの、貴重な天然資源から無価値の廃棄物への移項のエントロピックなそれにすぎぬとする考え方は、うれしいものではない。現に経済学者の大半はその経済モデルにエントロピーという視点を導入してはいない。

　プリゴジーンの着想[32]の応用篇として、資源の枯渇と環境汚染への怖れを減殺すべく、自己組織型の社会システムを通じてこのカオスの中から秩序が生まれてきうると考えている向きもある。[33] 日本のもつもっとも貴重な資源たる有能にして技能をもつ国民に、エントロピックな経済成長をスローダウンし、そうすることで物資非消費型の成長という健全なモデルを目指して汗を流してもらうことは、CO国家としての日本の責務といえるのではないか。

　それができないようなら、資源戦争が引きつづくだけである。

and at the end of the product life-cycle, dispose of them in waste sites scattered all over the land, we have transformed these materials from a state of availability and order to one of unavailability, disorder and chaos.

As Georgescu-Roegen, an unorthodox economist, said, and as I myself would say, what goes into the economic processes represents valuable natural resources and what is thrown out of it is valueless waste. But this qualitative difference is confirmed, albeit in different terms, by a particular branch of physics known as thermodynamics. From the viewpoint of thermodynamics, matter-energy enters the economic process in a state of low entropy and comes out of it in a state of high entropy.[31]

The idea that the economic process is an entropic one that proceeds from order to disorder and chaos, from valuable natural resources to valueless waste, is not a happy one. Most economists do not integrate ideas of entropy into their economic models.

Based on an adaptation of Prigogine's ideas,[32] some think that order might arise out of this chaos through self-organizing social systems so as to reduce fears of resource depletion and environmental pollution.[33] Perhaps it is to be Japan's challenge, as a Conscientious Objector nation, to demonstrate a self-organizing social system which takes its most precious resources, its gifted and skilled people, and puts them to work to slow entropic and economic growth and give us healthier models of non-material-consumptive growth. More resource wars await us if we are unable to do this

資源戦争

　自国の利益だと感じたときは、資源確保のためには征服や暴力にも訴えるというのが、歴史を通じての国家像であった。17・18・19世紀を通じ、イギリス、フランス、オランダなどの、ヨーロッパ諸国が植民地の拡張に向かったのも資源がその主たる要因であった。19世紀、金や鉱物資源や土地を求め、「明白なる運命」という旗印のもと西方へ移動しつづけていった白人が、先住アメリカ人の大量虐殺を事としたのも資源を求めてのことであった。日本が西欧のひそみにならって朝鮮や台湾、やがては中国へと手をひろげ、ついには東南アジアに入りこんでいったのも、天然資源という要素がつよかった。

　自分たちの資源ベースをあらかた使いはたしたこととて、いまや「豊かな」先進国は「貧しい」途上国に目を向けるに至った。ハイテク成長や消費エンジンを維持していくために不可欠な鉱物、燃料その他の原料のストックのうち、その多くについては、いまや途上国こそがその持ち分を増やしつつあるからである。

　湾岸戦争の場合に見たように、豊かで軍事的に強大な国家は、「自分たち」の不可欠な原料をひきつづき独占確保することが自国の利益に合致するとみなしたときには、軍事力に訴えることも辞さないのである。

　これらの消費や汚染にかかわる諸問題は、軍事力で対応することなどできっこない。のみならず軍隊自身、巨大きわまりない資源の消費者であり環境の汚染者なのである。軍事的な太いこぶしに支えられた植民地帝国主義のもつ傲岸不遜は、いまや国際的な行動型態としてとても受け入れられるものではない。

　プリゴジーンの所説をうんと楽天的に考えてみるなら、過剰消費や環境破壊をめぐるカオスの中から非暴力的な形で

Resource Wars

Throughout history nations have resorted to conquest and violence to secure resources that they felt were in their national interest. Resources were major factors in 17th, 18th and 19th century British, French, Dutch and other European colonial expansion, as was the practice of Native American genocide by the USA in its 19th century manifest destiny movement across the west in search of gold, minerals, and land. Following the lead of the West, Japanese expansion into Korea, Formosa, China, and ultimately into Southeast Asia, also had a strong resource component.

Today, having depleted much of their own resource base, the "rich" now look to the "poor," the developing nations, who hold increasing portions of the world's stock of minerals, fuels, and other raw materials essential for keeping the high technology growth and consumption engine running.

As we saw in the Persian Gulf war, the rich and militarily powerful do not hesitate to reach out with military force when it is deemed in their national interest to assure continued domination of what they consider to be "their" source of essential raw materials.

These consumption and pollution problems are ones that cannot be dealt with by military force. In fact, the military itself is one of the gargantuan consumers and polluters. The arrogance of colonialism and imperialism with a large military fist is no longer an acceptable form of international behavior.

In a most optimistic Prigoginian sense, perhaps "new-order" will non-violently arise out of the chaos of over-con-

「新秩序」が生まれ、豊かな国と貧しい国との拡大一方の格差に橋をかけ、組織のあり方という点でわれわれに生物の種としての新しい路線につくことを可能にしてくれるかも知れない。[34] この新しい方向性は、CO国家としての日本がGTBDという形での代替奉仕サービスを手がけることによって、さらに火が付くことも考えられる。

GTBD（設計によるグリーン技術）

アメリカやヨーロッパそれに日本といった第1世界の国々がこの機に応じて立ち上がり、より省エネ型で環境にやさしい技術を作り出すために科学技術面での専門的な知見を駆使する方向に向って指導性を発揮することに踏みこんでくれるようなら、資源戦争勃発の可能性を薄めることも可能である。この種の技術のことを私は、「設計によるグリーン・テクノロジー」と呼んでいる。先進国は自らのためにも、また途上国がもって範とすべきモデルとしても、これを実践していくべきである。CO国家としての日本は多くの面でGTBD上の貢献をなしうる、ユニークな資質に恵まれている。

技術者が手当てすべきすべての機能面での要件を満足させるばかりでなく、グリーン・テクノロジーとは、工学上の設計過程のごく当初から、すべての製品、製造工程、それに他のシステムにおいてあらかじめ省エネ低汚染を目指していることが前提となる。GTBDは、技術創成過程でもっと長期的なライフサイクルを視野に入れておくことを前提としており、理想的には原料の採掘から全生産工程を経て消費さらには廃棄物処理に至るまでの全ライフサイクルが考慮に入れられるべきである。

すでにスカンジナビア諸国やドイツ、オランダなどでは芽生えつつあり、アメリカではほんのわずか、日本ではある程

sumption and ecological destruction to help us bridge the widening chasm between the rich and the poor—so as to launch us as a species on a new path in terms of the way we organize ourselves.[34] This new direction might well be blazed by Japan as a CO nation doing alternative service in the form of GTBD.

Green Technology By Design

The likelihood of resource wars can be reduced if first-world countries, the USA, Europe, and Japan, will rise to the occasion and become responsible nations which provide leadership in the use of scientific and technical expertise to create orders of magnitude more resource-conserving, and environmentally benign technology. My name for this kind of technology is "green technology by design." Developed countries must do this for themselves, and as appropriate models for developing nations to follow. Japan is in many ways uniquely equipped to make a GTBD contribution as a Conscientious Objector nation.

In addition to satisfying all the other functional performance design criteria that engineers must address, green technology by design implies technology (all products, manufacturing processes, and other systems) that has been designed, from the very beginning of the engineering design process, so as to minimize resource consumption and pollution. GTBD implies that a much broader life-cycle perspective be brought to the process of technology creation—ideally, a life-cycle ranging from the extraction of raw materials through production, consumption and finally, to disposal. Although GTBD is starting to emerge in Scandinavia, the

度までは見られるようになったとはいえ、第1世界の国々でもこのGTBDなる工学的発想がまだ揺籃期にとどまっているのは残念である。[35]

　すべての先進社会そして途上社会にあっても、省エネしかも環境にとって安全な生存形態が先進国用に作り出され、途上国がより健全なモデルとして跡を追うことができるような、そういう目標を探究していく余地は、有能な人々の目前に大きく拡がっている。われわれ先進国の人間が手がけるべきことの1つは、どうしたら物質へのお互いの飽くなき欲望をへらす一方で、個人と社会の成長を育んでいけるような有意義にして充足感のある生存への途を見出すか、という点である。（われわれが目指しうる理想像については補遺の2を参照されたい）

ユニークな資質に恵まれた国、日本

　すでにして日本は、すこぶる高品質の自動車や弱電機器、小型の農業用トラクターその他、全世界の人々が生活の充実のために手に入れている製品を設計し製造するだけの能力があることを示している。

　アメリカの自動車メーカーや他の業界は、この種の高品質のシステムをどう設計し作り上げていったらよいかについて日本から多くのものを身につけた。長年にわたって私も主張してきたように、われわれに高品質の製品を与えてくれたと同じ道具だてや手法は、GTBDにも適用できる。

　日本のメーカーや技術者はわれわれに対し高品質の技術を物にする上に一番大切なのは、はじめからそのつもりで設計することに在ること、を知らしめてくれた。つまりは製品を考案する最初の段階から、設計上の重要な物差しとして品質と信頼性とを置く、という心構えである。このことを私は「設計による品質維持」QBDと呼んでいる。

Netherlands, Germany, a little in America, and some in Japan, unfortunately, this engineering concept is in its infancy in first-world countries.[35]

There exists a vast arena for exploration by gifted people in all advanced societies, and in developing societies as well, for less consumptive and environmentally safe modes of existence for rich nations, and as healthier models for developing nations to emulate. One of the urgent things that we in the developed countries must do is to face this huge challenge of how we might reduce our own large appetites for material things, and yet find a meaningful and fulfilling existence that enables a caring kind of personal and social growth. (See Appendix 2 for an ideal toward which we might strive.)

Japan Uniquely Equipped

Japan has already demonstrated its ability to design and manufacture very high quality automobiles, consumer electronics, small agricultural tractors, and hosts of other technology that people around the world buy to enhance their lives.

American automobile companies and many other US industries have learned a great deal from Japan as to how to design and manufacture these high quality systems. As I have argued for many years, the same tools and techniques that give us high quality products can be used to give us GTBD.

Japanese manufacturers and engineers have helped us to learn that the most important way to build high quality technology is to design it that way in the first place—that is, to place quality and reliability as important design criteria at the very beginning of product conception. This I call "quality by design" (QBD). QBD differs significantly from the past prac-

このQBDは、製造工程の中間もしくは最終段階で製品の品質検査を入れこむという従来のやり方、すなわち「品質管理[QC]」と呼びならわしてきたものとは大幅に異なっている。

　世間の常識とはちがい、QBDを重視することでより高品質の技術を、しかも低コストで達成することができることを、われわれは日本の体験から悟ったのである。この同じ理念を同工異曲的に採用し、技術創造のごく初めの段階で、省エネと環境面との優美さを、製品寿命の高齢化の可能性ともども重視してかかるなら、より低コストでしかも良質な環境を達成しうる、とあえて主張するものである。いま環境分野で幅をきかしている「パイプの最後の段階」での汚染制御方法に代わって、である。

　企業や政府にとって何が求められるかといえば、すべての新技術は、製品寿命という考え方に加えて、(1) 創造されるべき当該システムが地球資源の使用量を最小限に押さえつつ人間の必要を充たし、(2) 大気や水や土地や外部宇宙を汚染しない、という2条件を充たすことである。

　GTBDを推進することが、他国はともあれ、日本にとっての具体的な利益に合致するものであり、同時に環境と折り合いをつけることで将来の暴力的な争いの確率性を減らしていく上に世界規模での非暴力的な平和貢献たりうるかを示す、1つの明快な実例を以下にあげたい。

中国向けの技術

　中国がいつの日にかアメリカや日本やヨーロッパと同じ資源消費段階に手がとどいた際に、日本の環境がどのようなものになるかを、想像できるだろうか。中国に多量の技術を売却している日本は、中国向けならびに中国国内の技術開発に対し前向きの影響力を行使できる。国内の石炭資源が硫黄を

tice of trying to inspect quality into the product during or at the end of the manufacturing process—what we historically have called "quality control." From Japan we have learned that, contrary to conventional wisdom, it is possible to achieve higher quality technology often at lower cost by focusing on "quality by design." I argue analogously that if we but use this same philosophy and place resource conservation and environmental elegance along with an expanded life-cycle perspective at the beginning of technology creation, it may well be possible to achieve a higher quality environment, at less cost, than by the "end-of-pipe" pollution control methods that presently dominate our approach to the environment.

What is needed is for companies and governments to require that all new technology have two major additional design criteria along with a life-cycle perspective: (1) that the systems to be created must satisfy human needs while minimizing the use of earth's resources, and (2) that they must not pollute the air, water, land, or outer space. Let me give one clear-cut example of why it is in Japan's specific interest to do GTBD, and at the same time make a non-violent worldwide contribution for peace with the environment that will also minimize the probability of future violent conflict.

Technology For China

Can we imagine what the environment in Japan will be like if the Chinese ultimately reach the levels of resource consumption seen in the USA, Japan, and Europe? Japan sells much technology to China and has the potential to exert a positive influence on technology development for and in

ダムができたことで水没したアマゾンの森。（ブラジル、パラ州）
A forest inundated by the creation of a dam. (Pará, Brazil)

多量に含んでいるだけあって、中国としては来たるべき20年の間に今後の経済成長を支えるべくその石炭火力発電能力を2倍にすることを考えている。

　中国からの偏西風は発電の結果としての「外部不経済」を、大気にのせて日本列島の各地に拡がる住居や田畑、山々や森林、河川や住民に吹きつける。私がなぜこういった事情を知っているかといえば、1986年に6ヵ月という間、上海の火力発電所の風下に住んで仕事に就いていた体験があるからである。日本の技術者や科学者をして、発電や自動車製造のための汚染をもたらさないGTBDなど、中国向けの技術の開発にあたらせることは、絶対に日本の自己利益に見合っている。「汚ない」発電施設の代わりに、日本は低コストで非汚染型の発電機材の設計、製造、頒布に世界規模でのリーダーシップを発揮すべきである。むろん大幅にきれいな石炭を燃料とする発電技術も含めてである。

代替エネルギー源

　より清潔な石炭を燃料とする発電技術が短期的な重要性をもつのは事実だが、日本はその持てる科学技術面や製造販売面での独創性を働かせることで、さまざまな形でのクリーンなやり方を開発、人々がそのエネルギー需要を、最小限の汚染と有限な化石燃料資源を使い切ることなく、充たしていけるよう画っていくべきである。

　この美しいホシの究極のエネルギー源は、何といっても太陽である。[36] 風力からバイオマス、それに光電池(PV)に至る太陽熱がらみのすべての技術はこれを積極的に押し進めていく必要がある。その中でも、PVを使って太陽光線を電気に変えていく技術にとくに注目したい。PVの主たる構成要素

China. With its high-sulfur coal resources, China anticipates fueling its future economic growth with a doubling of its coal-fired electrical generating capacity over the next twenty years.

Prevailing winds blow from China over the Japanese islands, carrying electricity's airborne "externalities" to the homes, fields, mountains, forests, rivers, and people of Japan. I know of these things from having lived and worked for six months downwind from a Chinese power plant in Shanghai in 1986. It is absolutely in Japan's self-interest to set its engineers and scientists to the task of creating non-polluting GTBD for the production of electricity, automobiles, and all other technology sold to China. Japan's marketing experts must promote this kind of technology. Rather than selling "dirty" electrical generating equipment, Japan ought to take a major world-class leadership role in designing, manufacturing and distributing low-cost non-polluting generating equipment— including orders of magnitude cleaner coal-fired technology

Alternative Energy Sources

Important as is the short-term goal of cleaner coal-fired electrical generating technology, Japan ought to set its scientific, engineering, manufacturing, and marketing creativity to work on hosts of clean ways to enable people to satisfy their energy needs with minimum pollution and without depleting our finite supply of fossil fuels.

The ultimate source of energy on this beautiful planet is the sun.[36] All of the many kinds of solar technology, from wind to biomass to photovoltaics, need to be aggressively pursued. Let me focus on just one—photovoltaic (PV) direct conversion of sunlight into electricity. Silicon, the principle

たるシリコンは、もっとも豊富に地球上に存在する固体である。すでに日本はPV技術の開発において、主導的な役割を演じているが、さらに一層の努力をつぎこみ、この技術を経済的な競争力をもつ段階にまで高めることで、世界平和と公正ならびに環境との平和的な折り合いへの日本に独自な貢献の1つたらしめては、と思う。

PVのような再生可能エネルギーは、個人が集権化した電力パワーにつながっている必要がないという点で、本来的に民主的な存在といえる。発展途上の国々が、先進国のお互いがすっかりウケに入っていると同じ生活水準を享受しうる最低限ギリギリの可能性をもたらそうとするなら、これらのより良質な技術が何としても欠かせないのである。

原子力にはノーを

原子力がかかえている特異な問題の数々を思うと、私としてもどこの国であれ、原子力をもってその振興と輸出を目指すべき技術とするには腰が引ける。第一、原子力は手が届かぬほど高くつくし、再生可能なエネルギーのもつ分権的かつ配分的な性格と比べて本来的に非民主的である。それに加え、核兵器との関係が親密であり、高レベルの放射能を帯びた廃棄物の安全かつ受け入れ可能な処理方法が見当たらないことなどを思うと、そういわざるを得ない。

1995年に福井県の敦賀でおきた「もんじゅ」の事故はこれらの核システムのもつ危険性を端的にあらわにした。とくによくないのは高速増殖炉である。健康や環境への危険度がプルトニウムがらみでとくに高いのと、この技術のもつ核兵器との決定的な類縁関係とがその理由である。

日本は人間面技術面での技能と資源とを駆使して、自国ならびに世界の国々を、原子力エネルギー技術からできるだけ

ingredient in photovoltaic cells, is perhaps the most abundant solid element on planet Earth. Japan, already the leader in the development of PV technology, should intensify its efforts to bring this technology to the point of economic competitiveness, and let this be one of its contributions for world peace and justice, and for peace with the environment.

Renewable energy systems like PV are inherently democratic in that individuals no longer need to be connected to a centralized source of power. We need these better technology models if third-world countries are to have even the slightest chance of enjoying the standard of living of which we in the first-world have grown so fond.

No to Nuclear Power

Because of nuclear power's unique problems, its prohibitive expense, its inherently undemocratic nature as compared to distributed and decentralized renewable energy systems, its intimate connection with nuclear weapons, and because there seems to be no safe and acceptable way to dispose of high-level radioactive waste—I do not encourage nuclear power as a technology that any nation ought to promote and export.

The 1995 problem with the Monju fast-breeder reactor in Tsuruga, Fukui Prefecture, simply highlights these dangerous nuclear systems.[37] Breeder reactors are especially bad because of the massive health and environmental hazards associated with plutonium and because of this technology's absolute connection with nuclear weapons.

Japan ought to use its human and technical skills and resources to unhook itself and the rest of the world from

速やかに足抜けさせねばならない。

　これは、日本によるGTBDを通じての、世界平和と公正、環境との折り合いへの、いま1つの貢献たりうる。

註釈

1. デイドレー・メュレーン、既出書。

2. デビッド・サンガー「国連トップの助言、日本の批判をまきおこす」
　 ニューヨーク・タイムズ国際版、1993年2月7日号L17ページ。

3. モハンダス・K・ガンジー、既出書。

4. ジーネ・シャープ『非暴力行動の政治学』第5版。第1巻「権力と争闘」、
　 第2巻「非暴力行動の方法」、第3巻「非暴力行動の力学」。1984年　ボス
　 トン、ポーター・サージェント出版社刊。

5. ジーネ・シャープ『市民ベース防衛：脱軍事兵器システム』1990年　プ
　 リンストン、プリンストン大学出版局刊。

6. 国際連合憲章：国際司法裁判所法規19ページ。国連広報局、報告書リプ
　 リントUSA93166、1994年3月。

7. 人口報告インターナショナル（国際連合の付属機関）。ニューヨーク、
　 1995年。

8. マイケル・トビアス『第三次世界大戦、第2一千年期末における人口と
　 生物層』1994年　ニューメキシコ州サンタフェ、ベアー出版社刊。

9. 日本のODA要約。1996年。

10. 井上聖「援助という武器をめぐる綱引きはじまる　政策手段の喪失に
　　 される外務省」、日経ウィークリー、1995年12月11日。

11.「統合されつつある世界の働く人々：世界開発報告」世界銀行向け。
　　 1995年、オックスフォード大学出版局。1995年。

12. 上掲書、196ページ。

13. 木村一治、ジョン・M・カーペンター『核時代の50年を核とともに生き
　　 て。日本の物理学者の回想記』1993年　仙台、佐々木印刷出版刊。

nuclear energy technology as rapidly as possible. This can be another of Japan's GTBD contributions to world peace and justice and to peace with the environment.

NOTES

1. Mullane, Deirdre, (ed.), *Words To Make My Dream Children Live: A Book Of African American Quotations*. New York: Doubleday, 1995, p. 278.

2. Sanger, David E., "UN Chief's Advice Stirring Japanese Criticism." *New York Times International*, 7 February 1993, p. L17.

3. Gandhi, Mohandas K., "The Origins of Satyagraha Doctrine," in Sibley, Mulford Q. (ed.), *The Quiet Battle: Writings on the Theory and Practice of Non-Violent Resistance*. Chicago: Quadrangle Books, Doubleday Anchor, 1963.

4. Sharp, Gene, *The Politics of Nonviolent Action*, in three volumes: 1. *Power and Struggle*, 2. *The Methods of Nonviolent Action*, 3. *The Dynamics of Nonviolent Action*. Boston: Porter Sargent Publisher, 5th printing, 1984.

5. Sharp, Gene, *Civilian-Based Defense: A Post-Military Weapons System*. Princeton: Princeton Univ. Press, 1990.

6. Charter of the United Nations and Statute of the International Court of Justice, UN Department of Public Information, Reprint USA–93166, March 1994, p. 19.

7. Population Communications International, an affiliate of the United Nations, New York, 1995.

8. Tobias, Michael, *World War III: Population and the Biosphere at the End of the Millennium*. Santa Fe, NM: Bear & Co., 1994.

9. Japan's ODA Summary 1996/reference 4, *http:www.nttls.co.jp/infomofa/oda/sum1996/ref..4.html*.

10. Inose, Hijiri, "Tug-Of-War Develops Over Aid 'Weapon': Foreign Ministry Faces Loss of Policy Tool," *Nikkei Weekly,* 11 December 1995.

11. Table 18, Workers in an Integrating World: World Development Report— 1995, published for the World Bank, Oxford University Press, 1995.

12. Ibid. p. 196.

13. Kimura, Motoharu, with Carpenter, John M., *Living With Nuclei: 50 Years in the Nuclear Age; Memoirs of a Japanese Physicist*. Sendai, Japan: Sasaki Printing and Publishing Co., Ltd., 1993.

14. 豊田利幸「すべての核兵器を廃絶せよ」　ジャパン・タイムズ紙　1995年6月19日号ならびに「核軍縮を妨害する政治」同紙　1995年6月20日号。

15. デビット・ロンギ『非核の道　ニュージーランド方式』　オークランド、ニュージーランド、1990年　ペンギン叢書ニュージーランド版。

16. 「東南アジアの興隆とともに日本は同地域での役割を考え直す要」　日経ウィークリー誌、1995年12月12日号、1996年1月1日号。

17. トニー・ジロッテ「わが裏庭に核兵器は不要との東南アジア諸国の姿勢に米中両国憤激」　ザ・クリスチャン・サイエンス・モニター紙、1995年12月26日号7ページ。

18. ジョナサン・S・ランディ「米核兵器のあの新しいテスト方法ををめぐる激論」
ザ・クリスチャン・サイエンス・モニター紙、1997年1月15日号　1ページ。

19. リチャード・F・グリメット「第三世界への通常兵器の移転・1986年―1993年」　連邦議会調査局、ワシントンD.C.　1994年。

20. ルース・レガー・シヴァード「世界軍事社会支出　1991年」14版　世界優先順位、ワシントンD.C.、1991年。

21. シャープ　前出書。彼は最近台湾での講演でその考え方を述べた。「非暴力制裁」誌、第4巻、第4冊。アルバート・アインシュタイン研究所。
　　なお、1995年春、アルバート・アインシュタイン研究所は、シャープの着想の研究と応用を進め、さらには全世界の紛争について非暴力的な対応を考えていくために設立された。

22. チャールズ・M・オーバービー「持続可能な未来のための製品設計：倫理の問題として」アメリカ工学教育協会 (ASEE) 議事録。1980年年次大会、於ワシントンD.C.。

23. ホァン・マルティネツ＝アリエヤならびにクラウス・シュルプマン『生態学的経済学：エネルギー・環境・社会』1990年　英国オックスフォード、マサチューセッツ州ケンブリッジ、ブラックウェル出版社刊。

24. マーチン・オコナー（編）『資本主義は持続可能か：政治経済学と生態学の政治学』1994年　ニューヨーク、ロンドン、ギルフォード出版刊。

25. チャールズ・M・オーバービー　前掲論文。

26. タルボット・ページ『保存保護と経済効率：材料改策への1つの接近：未来への資源』3ページ。1977年　ジョンス・ホプキンス大学出版局刊。

27. ジェレミー・リフキン『エントロピー：新しい世界観』35ページ　1980年ニューヨーク・バイキング出版。

14. Toyoda, Toshiyuki, "Abolish All Nuclear Weapons," *Japan Times*, 19 June 1995, and "Nuclear Disarmament Stymied By Politics," *Japan Times*, 20 June 1995.

15. Lange, David, *Nuclear Free—The New Zealand Way*. Auckland, NZ: Penguin Books (NZ) Ltd., 1990.

16. "As Southeast Asia Blooms, A Need For Japan To Rethink Role In Region." *Nikkei Weekly*, 12 December 1995–1 January 1996.

17. Gillotte, Tony, "No Nukes in Our Backyard Stance By Southeast Asia Riles US, China," *The Christian Science Monitor*, 26 December 1995, p. 7.

18. Landay, Jonathan S., "Explosive Debate Over New Ways To Test US Nuclear Stockpile," *The Christian Science Monitor*, 15 January 1997, p. 1.

19. Grimmett, Richard F., Conventional Arms Transfers to the Third World, 1986–1993. Congressional Research Service, Washington, DC, 1994.

20. Sivard, Ruth Leger, *World Military and Social Expenditures 1991*, 14th Edition. World Priorities, Box 25140, Washington, DC, 20007, 1991.

21. Sharp, *Civilian-Based Defense*, op. cit.. p. 7.
Sharp recently presented his ideas on CBD policy in Taiwan. See "Civilian-Based Defense Policy Presented in Taiwan Lectures," *Nonviolent Sanctions*, Vol. VI, No. 4, Spring 1995. The Albert Einstein Institution, 50 Church St., Cambridge, MA 02138. The Albert Einstein Institution was founded to advance the study and use of Sharp's ideas, and in general to promote the use of non-violent action in conflicts throughout the world.

22. Overby, Charles, "Product Design For A Sustainable Future: A Matter of Ethics?" American Society For Engineering Education (ASEE), Proceedings, 1980 Annual Conference, Washington, DC.

23. Martinez-Alier, Juan, with Schlupmann, Klaus, *Ecological Economics: Energy, Environment and Society*. Oxford, England, and Cambridge. Mass: Blackwell Publishers, 1990.

24. O'Connor, Martin (ed.), *Is Capitalism Sustainable?—Political Economy and the Politics of Ecology*. New York, London: The Guilford Press, 1994.

25. Overby, Charles M., op. cit.

26. Page, Talbot, *Conservation and Economic Efficiency: An Approach To Materials Policy, Resources for the Future*. Johns Hopkins University Press, 1977, p. 3.

27. Rifkin, Jeremy, *Entropy: A New World View*. New York: Viking Press, 1980, p. 35.

28. ニコラス・ジョルジェスク=レーゲン『エントロピーの法則と経済過程』1971年　マサチューセッツ州ケンブリッジ　ハーバード大学出版局。

29. ケネス・E・ボールディング『二十世紀の意味：巨大な過渡期』1965年　ニューヨーク、ハーパー&ロー出版、コロフォン叢書。日本語は岩波新書所収（清水幾太郎訳）。

30. ハーマン・E・デイリー、ケネス・N・タウンゼンド「地洋価値づけする：経済、生態、倫理」マサチューセッツ州ケンブリッジ、マサチューセッツ工科大学出版部刊。

31. ニコラス・ジョルジェスク=レーゲン『エネルギーと経済学上の神話：機構分析経済についてのエッセイ集』。第三章「エントロピーの法則と経済問題」53ページ。1976年　ニューヨーク、パーガマン出版刊。

32. イリヤ・プリゴジーン、イザベル・ステンガーズ『混乱から秩序へ：ヒトと自然との新しい対話』。1984年　ニューヨーク、バンダム叢書。

33. マーチン・オコナー、上掲書、24ページ。

34. イリア・プリゴジーン、イザベル・ステンガーズ、上掲書。

35. チャールズ・M・オーバービー「設計によるグリーン・技術：持続可能な開発に向けての技術教育への新しいパラダイム」『持続可能に向けてのクリーンな技術と製品』所収。1995年　ニューヨーク、スプリンガー・ベルラーグ社刊。

36. ハーマン・シャー『太陽熱宣言：全エネルギー供給を太陽熱で充たす必要とその達成のために』。1994年　ロンドン、ジェイムス&ジェイムス出版刊。

37. カメロン・W・バー「原子炉事故で政治騒然の日本」。ザ・クリスチャン・サイエンス・モニター紙、1995年12月29日号、1ページ。

28. Georgescu-Roegen, Nicholas, *The Entropy Law and the Economic Process.* Cambridge, Mass: Harvard University Press, 1971.

29. Boulding, Kenneth E., *The Meaning of the 20th Century: The Great Transition.* New York: Harper & Row, Colophon Books, 1965.

30. Daly, Herman E., and Townsend, Kenneth N., *Valuing The Earth: Economics, Ecology, Ethics.* Cambridge, Mass: MIT Press, 1993.

31. Georgescu-Roegen, Nicholas, *Energy and Economic Myths: Institutional and Analytical Economic Essays,* Chapter 3, "The Entropy Law and the Economic Problem." New York: Pergamon Press, 1976, p. 53.

32. Prigogine, Ilya, and Stengers, Isabelle, *Order Out Of Chaos: Man's New Dialogue With Nature.* New York: Bantam Books, 1984.

33. O'Connor, Martin, op. cit., p. 24.

34. Prigogine, Ilya, and Stengers, Isabelle, op. cit.

35. Overby, Charles M., "Green Technology by Design: A New Paradigm for Engineering Education for Sustainable Development," in *Cleaner Technologies and Cleaner Products for Sustainable Development.* New York: Springer-Verlag, 1995.

36. Scheer, Hermann, *A Solar Manifesto: The need for a total solar energy supply ... and how to achieve it.* London: James & James Ltd., 1994.

37. Barr, Cameron W., "Reactor Snafu Leaves Japan Politically Hot," *The Christian Science Monitor,* 29 December 1995, p. 1.

生まれたときから戦争があった。……地球とのかかわりが転換期を迎えている今日、支配から協同へ、分裂からつながりへ、不安定から相互依存へと進化を移していくべきである。

There was war from the moment of birth.... At this turning point in our relationship with Earth, we work for an evolution: from dominance to partnership; from fragmentation to connection; from insecurity to inter-dependence.

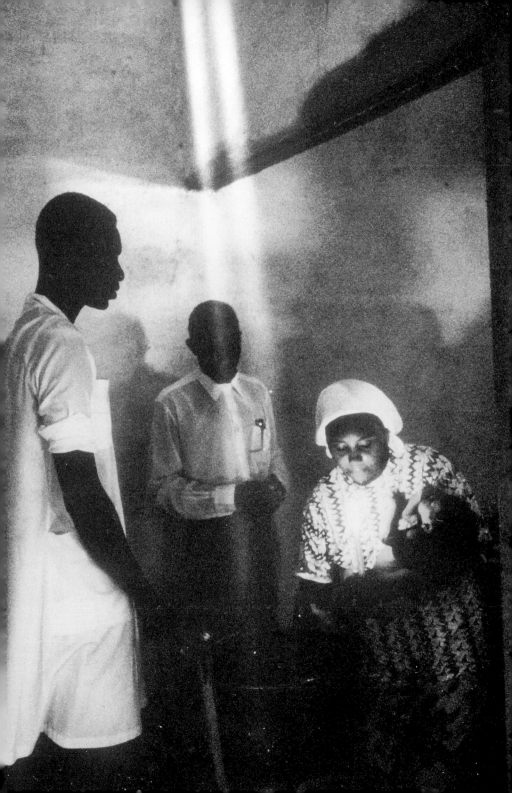

補遺 1

非軍事国日本が世界に貢献するために進むべき道；
朝日新聞の提案（1995年5月3日）

1. 国際協力法を制定し援助の充実を

　提言の第1は、非軍事の国際協力で世界の先頭に立つ日本が進むべき、具体的な道筋とそのあり方である。

　2010年の世界を想像してみよう。人口の激増と生活環境の悪化で、貧困と格差をめぐる対立が一段と先鋭化しているだろう。ほうっておけば地域紛争はますます増え、難民も急増しかねない。

　それを予防するためには、いまのうちに手をうつ必要がある。具体的には、平和と人権を世界に広げる日本国民の決意をうたいあげた「国際協力法」を制定するのだ。政府の途上国援助 (ODA) の質的改革を求めるとともに、非政府組織 (NGO) とあわせて車の両輪としたい。

2. 平和支援隊で従来型PKOに参加

　第2の提言は、「平和支援隊」の創設だ。将来に向けた「予防」策とともに、いま、現に、紛争や災害で人間的な暮らしを送れない人びとをどうするか。自衛隊とは別組織の平和支援隊は、そういう人道的な救援や災害救助のために敏速に動く。平和支援隊は同時に、非軍事の枠内に限って、国連の平和維持活動 (PKO) にも積極的に参加する。隊員の一部は護身用の小火器をもつが、平和支援隊は戦闘集団ではないから、その活動も正規の軍隊とはまったく違う。平和執行軍や多国籍軍に参加することもありえない。

Appendix 1

Proposal For A Nonmilitary Japanese Path Of Contribution To
The World; The Ashahi Shimbun's May 3, 1995

1. Enact an International Cooperation Law to upgrade external assistance.

Our first proposal charts in specific terms the course Japan should take
at the forefront of non-military international cooperation.

Let us imagine the world of 2010. With the living environment
being aggravated as a result of the population explosion, antagonism
over the issue of poverty and the gap in wealth among people would
have escalated in acrimony. If it is left unattended, regional conflicts
can proliferate and the number of refugees could increase dramatically.

To prevent this, remedial measures must be applied now. In
particular, an International Cooperation Law should be enacted that
expresses the resolve of the Japanese people to spread peace and
respect for human rights more widely in the world.

We also advocate qualitative improvements of our official development assistance—foreign aid—and reinforcement of the role of non-
governmental organizations in tandem as essential elements of such aid.

2. Create a Peace Support Corps for taking part in traditional peacekeeping operations.

Our second proposal is creation of a Peace Support Corps. Besides
taking preventive steps for the future, what else can be done for people who cannot live as humans because of conflict or natural disaster
now?

The Peace Support Corps—an entity separate from the Self-
Defense Forces (SDF)—would respond swiftly with such humanitarian relief and rescue operations in natural disasters.

The Peace Support Corps would also be an active part of United Nations peacekeeping operations in strictly nonmilitary areas.
Although some members of the corps would carry small arms for their
own protection, the corps' activities are completely different from those

3. 理想先取りの9条は改定の要なし

第3の提言で私たちは、自衛権に基づく自衛組織の保有を憲法は禁じていないとの立場を明確にしたうえで、現憲法、とくに9条の改定に強く反対する。

戦争や武力行使を放棄した9条は、人類の願いを率先してうたいあげた理想主義的な規範である。9条がつくった戦後日本の枠組み、なかでも「軍事が他に優先する」ことを否定した鉄則は、かけがえのないものだ。改憲で失ってはならない。

4. 自衛隊は国土防衛的な組織に改造

いわゆる専守防衛方の装備と編成に徹し、海外派兵は許されない。現在の自衛隊は、すでに許される自衛力の範囲を逸脱している疑いが濃いので、まず装備と隊員を削減し、あわせて目的、組織、編成などを全面的に改造する。

世界の戦略環境から見て、少なくとも来世紀初頭までは、日本が直接の侵略対象になる可能性は低い。中国や朝鮮半島など、不透明な要素は否定しきれないが、ソ連脅威論をもとに増強された冷戦型の現自衛力は大きすぎる。たとえば陸上自衛隊を段階的に半減したとしても、国の安全が直ちに損なわれることはない。むしろ、それが周辺国の軍縮の呼び水になれば、それだけ日本の安全度は高まろう。

of a regular army because the corps is not a combat force. Nor does it take part in peace-enforcement activities or in multilateral forces.

3. Idealistic Article 9 of the Constitution does not need to be revised.

In our third proposal, we express our strong opposition to revision of the present Constitution, especially its Article 9, after having clearly stated our position that the Constitution does not prohibit possession of self-defense force, based on the right of a nation to defend itself.

Article 9, which renounced war and use of force, is an idealistic norm that embodies the wish of mankind ahead of other nations. The framework that the Constitution set up for post-war Japan, especially the ironclad element of not giving precedence to military matters over other matters, is more precious than anything else. That principle must not be sacrificed by revision of the Constitution.

What, then, should be the organization for self-defense that is within the scope of the Constitution? The criteria and the limits of such an organization are presented in our fourth proposal.

4. Scale down the Self-Defense Forces into a force exclusively for defending the country.

The equipment and organization of such a force are to be strictly limited to defensive defense, and no combat troops would be sent abroad. Because there are strong reservations about the Self-Defense Forces as presently constituted overstepping the bounds of a force for self-defense, a considerable reduction in the SDF should be made, after which its mission, organization and make-up should be completely overhauled.

Given the strategic environment among the countries of the world, the likelihood of Japan being directly invaded is slight at least until early in the next century. Though there is no denying the uncertainties of China and the Korean Peninsula, the present SDF, organized in Cold War years and reinforced on the assumption of a Soviet threat, is too large. Phased reduction in personnel by half the present level in the Ground Self-Defense Force, for example, would not put the national security at immediate risk. And if such a reduction encourages arms reduction in neighboring nations, Japan's own security would be enhanced all the more.

5. 冷戦型から地域安保型重視へ転換

第5の提言は、アジアの平和のための組織づくりと日本の役割である。日米両国は冷戦型の安全保障体制を見直すこと、とくに在日米軍基地を撤去・縮小すること、そのうえで、予防外交や軍縮管理の機能をもつ欧州安保協力機構 (OSCE) 型組織が今世紀中にアジアでも発足できるよう、協力することが大事である。

6. 国連健全化をめざし改革の先頭に

最後に、日本は国連改革の先頭に立て、ということを具体的に提言したい。安保理事会の拒否権については段階的廃止を提唱し、また新常任理事国問題では、日独両国だけを論議の対象とするのではなく、アフリカ、アジア、中南米の地域代表3ヵ国もその対象とすべきであろう。

5. Overcome security arrangements for the Cold War and give emphasis to peace in Asia as a whole.

Our fifth proposal concerns establishing an organization for peace in Asia and Japan's role in creating it. It is important that Japan and the United States revamp the security arrangements that are oriented toward the Cold War, especially to dismantle or scale back the American military base presence in Japan. The two nations should make a concerted effort to establish an organization that would work for preventive diplomacy and arms control in Asia—similar to the Organization for Security and Cooperation in Europe—by the end of this century.

6. Take the initiative for reforming the United Nations into a healthier world body.

Last but not least, we would like to propose that Japan stand at the forefront of specific reform of the United Nations. We suggest that the veto powers for the permanent members of the Security Council be phased out and that discussion of the new permanent seats at the Security Council be made not merely for Japan and Germany but also for three other countries each representing Africa, Asia and Latin America.

補遺 2

デビッド・スズキ博士の相互依存宣言

カナダ、ブリティッシュ・コロンビア大学の遺伝学教授デビッド・スズキ博士は、相互依存についての哲学を明晰な形で明らかにしているが、CO国家としての日本が生態系という分野で、憲法第9条に催され、人間中心的で、世界規模のリーダーシップを発揮する上にあるいは参考になるかも知れない。スズキ博士とそのスズキ財団は、リオデジャネイロでの1952年の国連環境開発会議に向け、以下の相互依存宣言を起草すべく、数ヵ月を費やした。この短い宣言文は、数多くの言語に訳出されている。

相互依存宣言

われわれは知っている

われわれの養いとなる植物や動物を通じ、われわれが大地であることを。われわれの血管を流れる降雨と大洋であることを。われわれは大地の森林の呼吸であり、大洋の植物であることを。われわれはヒトという動物で、最初にめばえた細胞の子孫としての他のすべての生命とつながっていることを。われわれはこれらの仲間たちと共通の歴史を分かち合い、それが遺伝子に録されていることを。

われわれは不確実性に充ちた共通の現在を分かち合っていることを。われわれはまた、未だ明かされざる共通の未来を分かち合っていることを。

われわれヒトは世界を包むいのちのうすい皮膜をつむいでいる三千万もの種の1つにしかすぎないことを。生命あるものの世界の安定は、この多様性に依存していることを。このつながりの中で結び合わされたわれわれは、生命の基本的な要素を使い、洗滌し、共有し、補いあうことで互いにつながっていることを。われわれの故郷たる地球というこのホシは有限で、すべての生命がその資源と太陽からの光熱を分かち合い、したがって成長には天井があることを、そしてお互いがいまやはじめてその天井に触れたことを。

Appendix 2

David Suzuki's Declaration of Interdependence

Dr. David Suzuki, Professor of Genetics at the University of British Columbia, Canada, offers us a succinctly philosophy of interdependence, that might also be our guide for Article 9-driven, non-anthropocentric, world-class Japanese leadership in the ecosystem domain, as a conscientious objector nation. Suzuki and his David Suzuki Foundation spent many months drafting the following "Declaration of Interdependence" for the 1992 Rio de Janeiro UN Conference on Environment and Development. This brief statement has been translated into many languages.

Declaration of Interdependence I

THIS WE KNOW

We are the earth, through the plants and animals that nourish us. We are the rains and the oceans that flow through our veins. We are the breath of the forests of the land, and the plants of the sea. We are human animals, related to all other life as descendants of the firstborn cell.

We share with these kin a common history, written in our genes. We share a common present, filled with uncertainty. And we share a common future, as yet untold.

We humans are but one of 30 million species weaving the thin layer of life enveloping the world. The stability of communities of living things depends upon this diversity. Linked in that web, we are interconnected—using, cleansing, sharing, and replenishing the fundamental elements of life. Our home, planet Earth, is finite; all life shares its resources and the energy from the sun, and therefore has limits to growth. For the first time, we have touched those limits.

大気を、水を、土壌を、そして多様な生命を多くないが
しろにすることで、われわれが束の間の現在に奉仕すべく
限りなき未来から奪い去っていることを。これらのものを
拒みえても、それを変えることはできぬことを。

われわれは信ずる

　ヒトがあまりにもその数を増やしその手段があまりに
も強力となったが故に、われわれが生きる仲間たち
を絶滅に追いやり、大きな河川を汚し、古い樹木を斬り倒
し、大地や雨や風を毒性化させ、天空に孔をこぼったこと
を。われわれの科学は、喜びのみならず苦痛をももたらし、
何百何千万もの人々の苦難の犠牲においてわれわれの便宜
がはかられていることを。

　われわれは過去のあやまちから知恵を得、消え失せた仲
間を悼み、新しい希望の政治を作りつつあることを。きれ
いな大気や水や土壌を畏敬し、それが絶対に欠かせぬとい
う事実を尊重し、少数派を益しながらも、多数者の遺産を
縮小するような経済活動はあやまっていることを直視し、
環境破壊が生物学上の資産を喰いつぶす以上、開発にまつ
わるすべての計算には生態学社会学上のコストが勘案され
るべきことを。

　長い時の流れのなかにあっては、われわれなど束の間の
一世代にすぎず、未来を消し去る立場にはなく、知識にお
いて限りがある以上、われわれの後の世代のことを憶い、
慎重すぎるが故のあやまちはこれを甘受する。

われわれは以下のように決議する

　いまやわれわれが何を知り何を信じているかこそが、
お互いの生き方の基礎たるべきであり、地球とのか
かわりが転換期を迎えている今日、われわれは支配から協
同へ、分裂からつながりへ、不安定から相互依存へと進化
の歩を移していくべきである。

デビッド・スズキ：「変化のとき」15〜16ページ。1994年　カナダ、トロント、スト
ダート出版社刊。転載への許可は、1996年10月23日、オハイオ州アセントで、講演を
終わったあとスズキ博士により口頭で与えられた。

When we compromise the air, the water, the soil, the variety of life, we steal from the endless future to serve the fleeting present. We may deny these things, but we cannot change them.

THIS WE BELIEVE

Humans have become so numerous and our tools so powerful that we have driven fellow creatures to extinction, dammed the great rivers, torn down ancient forests, poisoned the earth, rain, and wind, and ripped holes in the sky. Our science has brought pain as well as joy; our comfort is paid for by the suffering of millions.

We are learning from our mistakes, we are mourning our vanished kin, and we now build a new politics of hope. We respect and uphold the absolute need for clean air, water, and soil. We see that economic activities that benefit the few while shrinking the inheritance of many are wrong. And since environmental degradation erodes biological capital forever, full ecological and social cost must enter all equations of development.

We are one brief generation in the long march of time; the future is not ours to erase. So where knowledge is limited, we will remember all those who will walk after us, and err on the side of caution.

THIS WE RESOLVE

All this that we know and believe must now become the foundation of the way we live. At this turning point in our relationship with Earth, we work for an evolution: from dominance to partnership; from fragmentation to connection; from insecurity to interdependence.

Suzuki, David, Time to Change, The Stoddart Pub. Co. Ltd., Toronto, Canada, 1994, pp. xv—xvi. Permission for publication orally granted to Dr. Overby by Dr. Suzuki, Athens, Ohio, 23 October 1996. after his lecture at Ohio University.

補遺 3

日本国憲法前文

　日本国民は、正当に選挙された国会における代表者を通じて行動し、われらとわれらの子孫のために、諸国民との協和による成果と、わが国全土にわたつて自由のもたらす恵沢を確保し、政府の行為によつて再び戦争の惨禍が起ることのないやうにすることを決意し、ここに主権が国民に存することを宣言し、この憲法を確定する。そもそも国政は、国民の厳粛な信託によるものであつて、その権威は国民に由来し、その権力は国民の代表者がこれを行使し、その福利は国民がこれを享受する。これは人類普遍の原理であり、この憲法は、かかる原理に基くものである。われらは、これに反する一切の憲法、法令及び詔勅を排除する。

　日本国民は、恒久の平和を念願し、人間相互の関係を支配する崇高な理想を深く自覚するのであつて、平和を愛する諸国民の公正と信義に信頼して、われらの安全と生存を保持しようと決意した。われらは、平和を維持し、専制と隷従、圧迫と偏狭を地上から永遠に除去しようと努めてゐる国際社会において、名誉ある地位を占めたいと思ふ。われらは、全世界の国民が、ひとしく恐怖と欠乏から免かれ、平和のうちに生存する権利を有することを確認する。

　われらは、いづれの国家も、自国のことのみに専念して他国を無視してはならないのであつて、政治道徳の法則は、普遍的なものであり、この法則に従ふことは、自国の主権を維持し、他国と対等関係に立たうとする各国の責務であると信ずる。
　日本国民は、国家の名誉にかけ、全力をあげてこの崇高な理想と目的を達成することを誓ふ。

Appendix 3

From the Japanese Peace Constitution Preamble

We, the Japanese people, acting through our duly elected representatives in the National Diet, determined that we shall secure for ourselves and our posterity the fruits of peaceful cooperation with all nations and the blessings of liberty throughout this land, and resolved that never again shall we be visited with the horrors of war through the action of government, do proclaim that sovereign power resides with the people and do firmly establish this Constitution. Government is a sacred trust of the people, the authority for which is derived from the people, the powers of which are exercised by the representatives of the people, and the benefits of which are enjoyed by the people. This is a universal principle of mankind upon which this Constitution is founded. We reject and revoke all constitutions, laws, ordinances, and rescripts in conflict herewith.

We, the Japanese people, desire peace for all time and are deeply conscious of the high ideals controlling human relationship, and we have determined to preserve our security and existence, trusting in the justice and faith of the peace-loving peoples of the world. We desire to occupy an honored place in an international society striving for the preservation of peace, and the banishment of tyranny and slavery, oppression and intolerance for all time from the earth. We recognize that all peoples of the world have the right to live in peace, free from fear and want.

We believe that no nation is responsible to itself alone, but that laws of political morality are universal; and that obedience to such laws is incumbent upon all nations who would sustain their own sovereignty and justify their sovereign relationship with other nations.

We, the Japanese people, pledge our national honor to accomplish these high ideals and purposes with all our resources.

訳者あとがき

　日本国憲法、特にその9条の戦争放棄条項に対し高い評価を吝まない外国人は、小生が個人的に知る限りでも、一人二人に留らない。今世紀最大の歴史家といわれるアーノルド・トインビー教授がそうだった。故若泉敬さんとの毎日新聞での長丁場にわたる対談で、人類の最先端を行くことの孤独に耐えながらも、あえてこの道をと、熱誠をこめて訴えたものだった。

　今世紀最大の生化学者でむろんノーベル賞受賞のA・セント＝ジェルジ博士もその『狂ったサル』の中で、憲法9条をもつ日本ぐらい世界で安全なところはない、と断じている。高名な文芸評論家で広島原爆乙女をアメリカに呼んでくれたノーマン・カズンズ氏、28歳で名門シカゴ大学総長となった哲学者のR・ハッチンズ博士、ノーベル平和賞を得たコスタリカのアリアス元大統領など枚挙にいとまない。徳孤ならず、なのだ。

　そしてこれらの人々は異口同音に、日本こそはその平和志向と科学技術力に経済力を加えて、人類社会のために画期的かつユニークな貢献ができるではないかと指摘、そのための構想を立ち上げるべきだと説きつづけた。その名を冠した国際的な奨学資金で知られるフルブライト元アメリカ上院議員もその1人だった。

　これらの先輩や知友に支えられ小生も「軍事力に代わる道義的代替案」（という不熟な表現）を合い言葉に、日本のできるまた果たすべき、非軍事面での寄与のあり方を唱えてきた。十数年前に出した『今日の問い、明日の答え』（アイペック社刊）はその模索を12人の外国人有識者と行なった共同作業であった。

　そして、いまわれわれは、憲法9条の会を発想創設した、チャールズ・オーバビー教授を有力な仲間の1人として持つにいたった。喜ばしくも力強いかぎりである。どうしたら憲法のもつ平和志向を、具体的な形で国際的に価値あらしむるものにできるか、を技術者出身の同教授は、冷静かつ客観的に説きすすむ。憲法問題が安保の再改訂やガイドラインの再検討をめぐって、にわかに再び浮上した今日だけに、著者の発言に聴くべき点は多いとせねばならない。

　原著者と訳者とのこの問題への篤い祈りと願いのすべてを賭けて、本書を英日対訳という形で読者の皆さんに送るものである。

1997年　夏
國弘正雄

ち きゅうけんぽう だい きゅうじょう
地球憲法第九条

A CALL FOR PEACE:
The Implications of Japan's War-Renouncing Constitution

1997年 8 月 1 日　第 1 刷発行

著　者　チャールズ M. オーバビー
翻　訳　國弘正雄
写　真　桃井和馬
発行者　野間佐和子
発行所　講談社インターナショナル株式会社
　　　　〒112 東京都文京区音羽 1-17-14
　　　　電話: 03-3944-6493 （編集）
　　　　　　　03-3944-6492 （営業）
印刷所　大日本印刷株式会社
製本所　黒柳製本株式会社

ISBN4-7700-2062-7

愛読者カード　　　　　　　　　　　地球憲法第９条

　今後の出版企画の参考にいたしたく存じます。ご記入のうえご投函くださいますようお願いいたします（平成11年８月１日までは切手不要です）。

a　ご住所　　　　　　　　　　　　　　〒□□□-□□

b　お名前　　　　　　　　　　　　c　年齢（　　　）歳

　　　　　　　　　　　　　　　　　d　性別　1男性　2女性

e　ご職業　　1大学生　2短大生　3高校生　4中学生　5各種学校生徒
　　　　　6教職員　7公務員　8会社員(事務系)　9会社員(技術系)　10会社役員
　　　　　11研究職　12自由業　13サービス業　14商工従事　15自営業　16農林漁業
　　　　　17主婦　18家事手伝い　19無職　20その他(　　　　　　　　　　　)

f　本書をどこでお知りになりましたか。
　　　1新聞広告(新聞名　　　　　)　2雑誌広告(雑誌名　　　　　.)
　　　3書評(書名　　　　　)　4実物を見て　5人にすすめられて
　　　6その他(　　　　　　　　　　　)

g　どんな本を対訳で読みたいか、お教えください。

h　どんな分野の英語学習書を読みたいか、お教えください。

御協力ありがとうございました。

郵 便 は が き

1 1 2

料金受取人払

小石川局承認

1285

差出有効期間
平成11年8月
1日まで

東京都文京区音羽一丁目

十七番十四号

講談社

インターナショナル　行

愛読者カード係

（地球憲法第9条）

★この本についてお気づきの点，ご感想などをお教えください。